Praise for Hilma Wolitzer's

The Company of Writers

"Writing is a lonely job, but Hilma Wolitzer points the way to the joys of a literary community. This is a good-hearted, witty, and most of all, a valuable book." —*Susan Isaacs*

"With humor and discernment, Hilma Wolitzer provides the be-ginning writer with the keys to the house of fiction—as well as useful advice about dealing with the dead ends, detours, and de-lays that are inevitable on the road to writing well."

—*Frederick Busch*

"As a writer and teacher of writing, I found much wisdom in this insightful and encouraging book. With her usual generosity, Hilma Wolitzer offers valuable suggestions about writing in solitude and about being part of a writing community."

—*Ursula Hegi*

"Reading *The Company of Writers* is like spending an evening in Hilma Wolitzer's living room, surrounded by all of her writer friends. Here, a writer finds kindred souls to laugh and commis-erate with, all while being in the charming company of Hilma herself, who is, as always, gracious, encouraging, honest, and wise. What a treasure." —*Robert Olen Butler*

PENGUIN BOOKS

The Company of Writers

Hilma Wolitzer is the author of six adult novels, including the best-seller *Hearts, Ending,* and *Tunnel of Love,* and four young adult novels. She has taught in the writing programs of several universities, including the University of Iowa, New York University, and Columbia, and for twenty years was on the faculty of the Bread Loaf Writers' Conference, where her lectures have been among the conference's most popular events. Her honors include Guggenheim and National Endowment for the Arts Fellowships; an Award in Literature from the American Academy of Arts and Letters; and the Barnes & Noble Writer for Writers Award, presented by Poets & Writers, Inc. Hilma Wolitzer lives in New York City.

The Company of Writers

Fiction Workshops and Thoughts on the Writing Life

Hilma Wolitzer

Penguin Books

PENGUIN BOOKS
Published by the Penguin Group
Penguin Putnam Inc., 375 Hudson Street,
New York, New York 10014, U.S.A.
Penguin Books Ltd, 27 Wrights Lane, London W8 5TZ, England
Penguin Books Australia Ltd, Ringwood, Victoria, Australia
Penguin Books Canada Ltd, 10 Alcorn Avenue,
Toronto, Ontario, Canada M4V 3B2
Penguin Books (N.Z.) Ltd, 182–190 Wairau Road,
Auckland 10, New Zealand

Penguin Books Ltd, Registered Offices:
Harmondsworth, Middlesex, England

First published in Penguin Books 2001

1   3   5   7   9   10   8   6   4   2

A portion of this work first appeared in different form
in *The New York Times.*

Grateful acknowledgment is made for permission to reprint "Block"
from *Carnival Evening: New and Selected Poems 1968–1998* by
Linda Pastan. Copyright © 1998 by Linda Pastan. Reprinted by
permission of W. W. Norton & Company, Inc.

LIBRARY OF CONGRESS CATALOGING-IN-PUBLICATION DATA
Wolitzer, Hilma.
The company of writers : fiction workshops and thoughts on the
writing life / Hilma Wolitzer.
p.   cm.
ISBN 0 14 02.9200 4
1. Fiction—Authorship.   2. Fiction—Authorship—Congresses.
I. Title.
PN3355.W652001
808.3—dc21   00–033629

Printed in the United States of America
Set in Fenice
Designed by Sabrina Bowers

For Amanda "Binky" Urban,
a writer's best friend

Contents

Contents

Part Two
Focus Sessions

Introduction

Writing fiction is a solitary occupation, but not really a lonely one. The working writer's head is virtually mobbed with characters, images, and language, making the creative process something like eavesdropping at a party for which you've had the fun of drawing up the guest list. Loneliness usually doesn't set in until the work is finished and all the partygoers and their imagined universe have disappeared. Doubt tends to creep in then, too. Is this story finished? Does it work? How can I tell? Will anyone want to read it? Most writers' hearts are divided by ambition and self-doubt. Even Virginia Woolf pondered, about her manuscript of *To the Lighthouse*, "Is it nonsense, is it brilliance?"

I remember completing a draft of my first short story and

wondering if it was any good—if it was, in fact, a bona fide story. Reading it over and over again didn't resolve my uncertainty. I desperately needed some feedback, but like many new writers, I didn't have a community of peers to turn to for an informed and objective opinion. At the time, I was a typical sixties housewife, deeply involved in the minutiae of daily household life. Most of my creative energy was spent on homemaking. I never made a simple tuna-fish sandwich for my children. They got to cannibalize tuna-fish men with carrot-stick limbs, green-pepper hats, and bulging olive eyes. Birthday cakes—made from scratch, of course—were decorated to the point of collapse, and my Jell-O molds were famous for their originality and complexity (one with diagonal stripes was considered my masterpiece). Years later, my older daughter confessed that she would much rather have worn a store-bought princess costume to the third-grade Halloween party than the witty headless horseman getup that garnered her first prize.

As a late bloomer, I'm sometimes asked if my husband or children felt abandoned or betrayed by my sudden new career. Frankly, I think the whole family was *relieved* when I took up writing and directed all that energy and inspiration elsewhere. Still, I didn't know where that first story came from (although the opening line—"Today a woman went mad in the supermarket"—might have given me a clue) or what in the world to do with it. So I asked my literate psychologist husband what he thought, and wisely, he suggested I seek professional advice, which led to my taking a writing workshop at a local college. There, for the first time, I found the company of other writers. Stanley couldn't have been any happier to have found Livingstone.

Community support has always been important to the budding writer. When he was twenty-six, Anton Chekhov wrote to D. V. Grigorovich, an older, established novelist, who had praised and encouraged him: "If I have a gift that should be respected, I confess before the purity of your heart that hitherto I have not respected it." And George Sand hung out with the likes of Balzac and Flaubert, from whom she solicited criticism, even of her published work.

But most aspiring writers aren't that well connected, and seeking help with your work from nonwriter spouses and friends can be disastrous, or at least unhelpful. People who love you tend to love your work simply because it's yours. Didn't your mother proudly display all your early artistic efforts on her refrigerator door? The average person, even among the intelligent and well-read, isn't qualified to offer constructive literary criticism. You're likely to get wrongheaded and conflicting suggestions from well-meaning friends: "Kill off the villain." "No, no, kill off the *hero*." And those with hidden agendas of competitiveness or downright envy might try to sabotage both your confidence and your burgeoning career. Remember Gore Vidal's candidly mean-spirited observation: "Whenever a friend succeeds a little something in me dies." Or my grandmother's: "With friends like that, you don't need enemies."

Bringing your work home, so to speak, can be very bad for personal relationships. Another member of your household may be put into the untenable position of live-in critic—a kind of damned if you do and damned if you don't predicament. And, watch out, he might be planning to show you something *he's* written, for which he is counting on reciprocal love. A fairly common, and safe, comment in those circumstances is, "This is terrific, sweetheart. I couldn't put it down!" How would anybody *dare* to put it down with you standing right there, wringing your hands and silently moving your lips during the reading? You must ask yourself if you really want an honest opinion from a loved one. The (soon to be ex-) wife of a popular novelist once complained about his habit of asking her to read a chapter of his work-in-progress at bedtime. "If I say I like it," she said, sighing, "he wants to know how much, and, in minute detail, exactly why. And if I *don't* like it, he's so disappointed, I have to cheer him up. In either case, we don't get to sleep for hours." She had my sympathy, but so did he. When I recount last night's dream for my husband at breakfast, I secretly want him to *admire* it, not analyze it.

To get some useful, unbiased criticism, and perhaps save your own marriage in the bargain, you can take your manuscript to a writers conference. Several excellent ones convene around the country. But they can be expensive and they generally meet for just a few days, therefore providing only a temporary solution. Toward the end of most of the conferences I've attended, students show signs of becoming bereft at the idea of parting from one another and their workshop. Like lovers separating after a summer romance, they swear to keep in touch forever. Some of them arrange to exchange manuscripts and criticism via the mail or the Internet. Others in need of the group dynamic decide to look into university writing programs. But for anyone who doesn't live near a university that offers regular workshops to nonmatriculating students, or for those who can't afford the tuition or who, like many of us, prefer a less formal setting, I suggest another, challenging but ultimately gratifying, option: start your own writing workshop.

"How?" they usually ask. This book is in answer to that question and to a few others, about reading and writing, that have come up in workshops over the years.

Part One

Your Literary Community

1

Getting Started

Men can starve from a lack of self-realization as much as they can from a lack of bread.

—Richard Wright

Before you do anything else, *you must acknowledge that you're a writer.* This may not be as easy as you think if you've never been published, and it may not even seem that important. Who really cares what you call yourself? But your identity as a writer is essential to the self-respect you'll need to perform well in a workshop, to give and receive criticism with confidence. In his autobiography, the Canadian novelist Robertson Davies declares, "I never became a writer: I was born a writer." When Carlos Fuentes was a child, he wrote, edited, and "published" a magazine, which was limited to a single copy that he also circulated himself. And in an interview, Katherine Anne Porter says, "I really started writing when I was six or seven years old." I suppose that before then she was a mere dilettante.

I started writing when I was a child, too, mostly dreadful poems about being blind, an unwed mother, or a refugee—I hadn't yet been told to write about what I know—and I wrote short fiction during my adolescence and the early years of my marriage. But until I sold my first story, when I was in my mid-thirties, no one ever referred to me as a writer, although a few people allowed that I had an "interesting hobby." Even my own parents, who took a burning interest in almost every other aspect of my life, hardly ever inquired about my progress on the literary front. Writing was something cute and clever I'd done as a kid, and something harmless I was still doing as a grown-up. I kept on writing, ardently and every chance I got, but I was almost as hard-pressed as they were to think of myself as a writer. I even devalued my personal experience. By then I *had* been advised to write about what I know, and I'd pick up a book at random and read the dust jacket bio: "Lance King is 27 years old. He's been a bush pilot, a molecular biologist, a short-order cook, an Olympic swimmer, and a translator of Sanskrit. This is his fifth novel." Well, no wonder he's so prolific, I'd think—look at all the *things* he knows. I figured he'd read Thomas Hardy, who said that the real purpose of fiction is "to give pleasure by gratifying the love of the uncommon in human experience." Compared to Lance King, I didn't know anything, or at least anything "uncommon" enough to be transmuted into fiction. If I had only known I was going to take up writing, I certainly would have lived a more interesting life.

Following publication, though, my work, with its modest scope and persistent domestic themes, took on an authenticity it had never had before. After my first short story appeared in the *Saturday Evening Post* (one of the more popular magazines of the time), I received congratulatory notes and phone calls from people I hadn't heard from in years, and a few I'd never even met. Some distant cousins hadn't bothered to read the story; they were just knocked out by seeing my name in print. Well, so was I! I remember going into the bathroom, locking the door, and trying on a series of scarves to see if I *looked* any different now, more artistic or bohemian—in essence, like a writer. My usually low-keyed father was thoroughly impressed by the authority of publication, too. "The *Saturday Evening Post!*" he exclaimed when I told him they'd taken the story, "Why, I read that at the dentist's!" The quality of my writing hadn't changed, but my status in the world surely had. I was even able to make a substantial down payment on my first car with the check from the *Post*—a brand-new 1966 Rambler station wagon—after living in the suburbs for six years without any means of transportation.

It's not surprising that one's unpublished scribbles don't really register with most people as a serious enterprise. After all, would you consider someone an actor if he's never received a callback, or recognize a composer whose work is played only inside his own head? And writing is one of the few professions you can pursue in your bathrobe and slippers, a uniform that doesn't exactly command respect. To make matters worse, almost everyone you meet *wants* to write, and absolutely everyone has a terrific story to tell. Wherever I go, it seems, someone sidles up like a thief in an alley with hot diamonds to unload and offers to share a best-selling idea based on a true experience. "You just have to write it down," they all say, "and we can split the profits." If they were writers they'd know that there usually *aren't* any profits, and they'd realize that one doesn't ever simply "write it down." As the fabled sportswriter Walter "Red" Smith once said, "There's nothing to writing. All you do is sit down at the typewriter and open a vein."

But the most vital difference between you and those dreamers is that you've actually *written* something, which you hope to improve before you go on to write something else. *It's what you do.* You may be a housewife, mother, father, doctor, teacher, or assembly-line worker, but you also fit *Webster's Dictionary* definition of a writer: "One who writes, esp. as an occupation." Notice that it doesn't say *primary* occupation. Joining a workshop—which implies that you're working at something—will bring further validation.

Don't give up your day job yet, but don't disparage it, either. To begin with, it will help to support this persistent writing habit of yours—most published writers need a supplemental income. After I sold that first story, which took me about half a day to write and netted me that Rambler wagon, I thought I'd lucked into a veritable cash cow. I couldn't help daydreaming: If I wrote a story a week, or even one a month . . . As a friend wryly predicted, I'd have a whole *fleet* of Ramblers before long. The sorry truth is that I didn't sell another story for more than three years, and that was to a small literary magazine for a fee barely big enough to buy a tankful of gas for my car. When Toni Morrison was asked in an interview what equipment a writer needs, she promptly replied, "Patience and a job." Morrison herself worked for years as an editor at a major publishing house.

There are other reasons, besides money, to dirty your hands with something other than ink and develop muscles beyond those in your fingertips. A job may provide fodder for your fiction as well as food for your table. Think of Melville's travels on a whaling ship and Charlotte Brontë's tenure as a governess. It's safe to say that Dickens's blacking-factory experience contributed to his compassion for the underdog and that Kafka's days spent as a lowly clerk fed his fear and loathing of authority. His most famous short story, "The Metamorphosis," may offer the best excuse ever for not getting to the office on time. Maxine Kumin raises horses; Ralph Ellison was, at various times in his life, a newsboy, a dental assistant, a receptionist, a jazz trumpeter, and a professional photographer; and Chekhov, William Carlos Williams, and Celine were all practicing physicians. I can't help thinking of the oddly lyrical beauty of medical language—membrane, delirium—and the possibilities it presents for metaphor. A doctor palpates for a "thrill" in a patient's pulse and notes the "quickening" of an unborn fetus. And then there's the rippling alliteration of tetany, tendinitis, torticollis! Carpenters have their plumb bobs and caliper rules; physicists study pulsars and quasars and quarks. When I was writing a scene in which the heroine-poet has her horoscope read, I decided to have my own chart done, too, strictly for research. I still don't believe in astrology, but both my character and I were taken by the language of the stargazers—such heavenly words as cusp and constellation. Every profession, it seems, offers the opportunity to enrich one's literary vocabulary.

Norman Mailer once said that writing books is the closest men ever come to childbearing. The writer's gestation may more closely resemble an elephant's, but like childbearing, the process is filled with unmistakably human pain and happiness. Much of domestic life has a similar richness for the fiction writer to mine; each unhappy family is still unhappy in its own fascinating way, and the larger political and social picture is reflected, in miniature, in the workings of the household. Jane

Austen's novels, for instance, focus on domestic arrangements, particularly on the fate of marriageable young women. No wonder, since women in Georgian England could not inherit from their parents (only their brothers became heirs). They either had to marry, or live off the generosity of a male relative who *had* inherited, or apprentice themselves in some menial, low-paying trade. The impact of these patriarchal constraints is implicit in Austen's work, even if it's not spelled out; large facts and ideas inscribed on a small canvas.

To the distress of some feminists, among whose numbers I count myself, I used to compare writing stories with cleaning out my closets. In both instances I was trying to make order out of chaos—in one, by discovering and organizing what was in the back of my mind, and in the other, by discovering and rearranging what was on the backs of my shelves. Editing a manuscript to trim its excesses was not unlike plucking out those stray wire hangers and single socks. I confess that now I'm a lot less preoccupied by household chores (or analogies). I haven't made Jell-O in decades, not since a spectacular pink-and-green arrangement I was unmolding for dinner guests slithered down the kitchen drain. Like Dorothy Parker, I decided not to eat anything more nervous than I am. But Jell-O appears in every one of my books, as an homage to my domestic past. And because it's colorful, shimmery, and layered with surprises, it makes a perfect all-purpose metaphor. Whatever *you* do in your "real" life may also be distilled into fictional material. Despite Hardy's edict about the "uncommon" in fiction, I now believe that *all* experience is extraordinary in some ways. It's just a matter of recognizing its literary potential.

Like many readers, I particularly enjoy books about working-class people, which let me in on the otherwise unknowable life of the elusive "other." The domestic staff laboring "downstairs" in Henry Green's *Loving*, the gas-meter reader in Chuck Wachtel's *Joe, the Engineer*, and the baby nurse in Dorothy Parker's short story "Horsey" are all made sympathetic as much by what they do as by who they are. Although I didn't think much of it at the time, I'm glad now that, prior to my marriage and to my life as a writer, I worked in a couple of offices and factories. Aside from gathering information in those places on how the commercial world works, I received some on-the-job training in human psychology and survival. Waiting tables one summer, I learned about the politics of power *and* about the heft of a loaded tray of dishes. If fiction teaches one how to live, it's conversely true that living teaches one how to write fiction. Those conventional jobs also accustomed me to some healthy work habits. Secretaries and assembly-line workers are compelled to keep regular hours, whereas writers, especially those without deadlines or a publisher in sight, may not be. Someone who's used to getting up at the same time every day, and following a regular schedule of work and play, will be better able to discipline himself when it comes to writing.

It's a good idea to find a private and comfortable place to work, at home if you have the space, and elsewhere if you don't. Gertrude Stein wrote her Cambridge lecture sitting on the fender of a car, but most of us would find that inconvenient. Many large cities have cooperative "writers rooms," where for a modest fee you can rent a cubicle, if not an entire room, of your own, or you might be able to sublet desk space for certain designated hours in an office building. A place to write doesn't have to be fancy or professional looking. Annie Dillard even advises against luxurious accommodations: "Appealing workplaces are to be avoided. One wants a room with no view, so imagination can meet memory in the dark." She also says: "You can read in the space of a coffin, and you can write in the space of a tool-shed meant for mowers and spades." They both sound a little cramped to me, but at least there's only room for *one* person in each of those places, so they'd be havens of privacy.

When I began writing, we lived in a small house, and my husband and I typed at opposite ends of the kitchen table—like Ferrante and Teicher at their twin pianos—while the kids and the dog romped noisily around us. I hadn't heard about Proust's cork-lined chamber yet, and I didn't have Colette's Willy to lock me up. I hadn't even begun to develop my subsequent neurotic need for peace and quiet. But a few months after my older child left home, I realized that I didn't have to preserve her room as a shrine to her childhood. I kept some of her posters on the walls for a while, and I still referred to the place as "Nancy's room," but eventually it became my office. I staked a claim to it by putting in extra bookshelves and a desk and by hanging a Keep Out sign on the door, the way my daughter had as a teenager. I was way past my own adolescence, of course, and even too old to join the literary brat pack, but I'm happy to report that fiction writing isn't an ageist profession. I've sometimes billed myself as "the Great Middle-aged Hope" because I published my first novel when I was in my mid-forties. But compared to Harriet Doerr, who published her first book in her mid-seventies, I was practically a child prodigy. Helen Hooven Santmyer came up with the best-selling *And Ladies of the Club* when she was in her *eighties* (and living in a nursing home); Doris Grumbach and Hortense Calisher are still going strong in their eighties; and James Michener was writing right up to the end of a long, exceedingly productive life. You don't need good legs to be a writer, only talent and perseverance.

Once you've allowed that you're a writer, with the right stuff, good work habits, a place to use them, and something to say, it will be much easier to find other closet writers in your neighborhood, perhaps even among your own friends and acquaintances. If you mention writing to your dentist, he may start spouting his latest sonnet while you're lying helpless in his chair, and at least one checker in your supermarket must keep her collected stories stashed under the till. In one of my favorite *New Yorker* cartoons, a portly man is staring blankly into a kitchen cabinet jammed with pages. The caption is his matronly looking wife's deadpan remark: "The gin is above the refrigerator. That's my novel."

Try striking up a literary conversation with people you've discussed books and movies and plays with before and whose opinions you respect, even when you don't agree with them. Mention that you've been writing, and other writers might feel comfortable enough to come out, too. Bring up some of the problems of process—how hard it is to find the time and solitude to work, how frustrating it's been to write in a vacuum—and see if a sympathetic discussion evolves. Broach the subject of getting together to exchange work, and ask if anyone happens to know of anyone else in a similar situation. Scout reading clubs, which have become so popular lately; although the inverse isn't necessarily true, most writers are passionate readers.

Articles in *Cosmopolitan* used to advise single women in search of men to hang out in hardware stores and auto-body shops. Similarly, writers in search of writing soul mates might find them lurking in bookstores or libraries; some libraries even provide desk space for writing. Fiction writers require a surprising amount of factual material for their stories, so you might ask the reference librarian if anyone has confided an interest in joining a workshop. Post a notice in your supermarket, on the library bulletin board, and at a couple of bookstores. Sample: "Fiction writers wanted for self-propelled workshop. Publication not required, but serious commitment is." If necessary, place an ad in a local newspaper. Advertising, of course, is much chancier than inviting people you've already met, sort of the bookish equivalent of a personals ad, and you'll certainly want to avoid deadbeats and serial killers. A brief telephone conversation and a submitted manuscript will usually determine compatibility or the lack of it. You might ask how long the person has been writing, which writers she particularly admires, and if she's participated in other workshops or book-discussion groups. I would be most receptive to candidates who read eclectically, because they are more likely to be knowledgeable and open-minded about writing that's different from their own.

As for manuscripts, ask for recent work, and look for evidence of talent, but not perfection. A perfect writer wouldn't *need* a workshop. Someone may submit a very polished *New Yorker*-type story, but one that lacks true feeling and conviction. Or a story may be carelessly written but still reveal a knowing and sympathetic sensibility. Both of these imperfect efforts would be excellent material for a workshop. I'd even take on a writer if his manuscript is generally a mess, but has a single brilliant passage. The workshop is something like Oz—not really a magical kingdom, after all, but a place in which to seek one's own creative heart or brain, or at least the courage to keep pursuing the writer's craft. On the other hand, you might receive a manuscript without any redeeming qualities or promise or, worse, no manuscript at all. Anyone who says he's always wanted to write but never got around to it is not a promising candidate for a workshop. Nor is someone who says she just wants to express herself or improve her communication skills, that is, become a better letter writer or conversationalist. It's difficult to reject people, especially when you yourself feel so vulnerable to rejection, but it's essential to have a group that can work well together. And it's best to find out before the workshop meets.

There are also some practical considerations in deciding who joins the group. You should all live near enough to one another, or the place(s) you'll meet, to avoid any hardships of transportation. Everyone should be available the same night of the week and be committed to showing up regularly. It would be great if everyone had equal artistic ability, but that's highly unlikely, and difficult to determine, anyway, from only one writing sample. It's more important that the level of criticism be constant (and high), which is fairly easy to ascertain from a simple conversation on the subject. Don't expect to agree on everything, but look for intelligent and stimulating disagreement.

Although you all have a common goal—to become better writers—other kinds of homogeneous groupings aren't recommended. A gender mix and a variety of age, ethnicity, and personality can add depth and texture to a fiction-writing workshop, and you might be surprised by the universality of most human experience. But what about other kinds of writers, such as poets or memoirists? I think it's best to limit admission to fiction writers because different criteria are employed to criticize other forms of writing, and not everyone will feel qualified to comment. *Reading* in other forms can really be instructive, though (more about that in chapter 3), and members of the group should be able to solicit responses to an occasional poem or essay of their own.

Each person invited to join the workshop is likely to suggest other possible candidates, and so on. The same screening process should be used for everyone, even highly recommended or well-published writers. And be careful of overzealousness in recruiting participants. This is not the army, and limits must be placed on the size of the group. I've found that between eight and twelve people function together most harmoniously. That range allows for a lively discussion, even when there are a few absences or dropouts, without sacrificing that invaluable sense of intimacy.

Finally, your group is formed and plans are made to meet. As the analyst says at the end of Philip Roth's *Portnoy's Complaint*, "Now vee may perhaps to begin."

2

Getting Together

Every writer I can think of was at some time a member of a group, whether it was the Greek agora, or the Roman bath, or the French Cafe, or the English University.

—John Ciardi

Some private writing groups decide to hire a professional leader, or their members are recruited by one. They feel that they need an organizing force, and find it reassuring to know that someone experienced is in charge. An effective workshop leader is egalitarian, generous, and inspiring, someone who encourages rather than dictates, and who never imposes his own vision and voice on others. But engaging such a person may be too costly for your group, or too reminiscent of the formal classroom. And it may be difficult to find a qualified leader in your area. In John Gardner's opinion, "Even in the best writers workshop one is likely to learn more from one's fellow students than from one's teacher."

There can also be certain unfortunate tendencies in a workshop with an official leader—even a good one—like writing to please that person in authority or hastening to agree with his opinions instead of forming one's own. Certain leaders seem naturally to attract adoring groupies, and I'm reminded of jurors being persuaded by a charismatic foreman's argument, against all the prevailing evidence. The courtroom often seems like an apt metaphor for a workshop, where manuscripts are, in effect, being tried. Yet a leaderless workshop can get completely out of hand, with everyone talking at once, or one or two members dominating the discussion. And no one has the mandate to lead the group away from a potentially combustible or destructive situation.

At the first session of that first college workshop I joined, led by Anatole Broyard, a writer who later became a prominent literary critic, he called on me to read my story aloud to the group (of about forty!—much too large for the purpose). Caught off guard, I had to spit out my chewing gum and stumble to the front of the room, dropping pages on the way. I was so nervous I almost hyperventilated, and I read with all the dramatic expression of a robot; I might have been reading my laundry list aloud. When Anatole asked the class to respond to my story, a man in the back of the room promptly pronounced it the most boring thing he'd ever heard. That was about all I cared to hear. I was ready to pack it in, to go home and just make Jell-O molds and tuna-fish men for the rest of my life, but Anatole slipped me a note, even as he told my detractor that he had every right to dislike my story, but he had to say *why* he found it boring and what I might do to make it better. And wasn't there anything in it he'd liked? The last thing I wanted at that moment was *detailed* negative criticism or even being thrown a bone of praise, but I half listened, anyway, as I surreptitiously opened the note, which I still have and still look at occasionally for reassurance. It said: "The story is fine. Congratulations. See me later."

Those words tempered the sting of the harsh ones the man in back was still offering, and in that moment I learned the most important thing about teaching writing. *There must be a balance of honesty and charity in the workshop.* Everyone must be aware of a feeling human being behind the work being discussed, and criticism has to be *useful,* not just derogatory or laudatory. As a fellow student once said in apt paraphrase, "We're not here to bury Caesar *or* to praise him."

When writers get together without any previous attachments to one another, it's sort of like a pickup basketball game (yet another handy metaphor for the workshop). If someone you've just met misses the basket, you're not apt to yell "Stupid klutz!" and you certainly wouldn't say "Great shot!" A more appropriate and effective response might be "Good try," with its implicit encouragement to try again. The object of the basketball players—besides winning—is to improve their game. The main object of a writing workshop is revision, not suicide, and a spirit of fellowship and mutual support can make that possible.

When I spoke to Anatole after class that first, fateful night, he suggested I join his advanced workshop, a much smaller group that met weekly in a conference room at the advertising agency where he worked during the day. This was more like it! I went home with buoyed self-confidence, and the following week I read the same story aloud again, with a lot more poise and expression this time, not to mention much higher expectations. To my disappointment, several members of the advanced group didn't like it, either, but at least their comments were balanced and constructive, and I was able to listen more calmly and to extract what I needed to improve the story. I'll always be grateful to Anatole for his intervention during that first class and for the years of mentoring that followed.

The lack of a constant, formal leader doesn't necessarily mean chaos or anarchy, though. In a subsequent, leaderless workshop I joined, we all sort of mentored one another. Members of the group took turns "leading" (from session to session), which entailed calling on people to read their work and on the others to comment, keeping things moving at a good pace and reinforcing those primary principles of honesty and charity. It might be encouraging to know that novelists Amy Tan, Ursula Hegi, Whitney Otto, Michael Cunningham, and Alice Hoffman have all participated in peer writing groups.

Private fiction workshops usually meet in members' homes, some groups always in the same home, because it provides the most comfortable space and the most privacy. If the meeting place is rotated, leadership may be rotated accordingly, but if you always meet in the same place, it's important to avoid a proprietary—"It's my ball, so you'll play by my rules"—attitude toward the workshop. Allow two to three hours for each session; two or three manuscripts may be properly discussed during that time. You'll want to establish a democratic process and a friendly atmosphere early on, but you will definitely need structure and a few firm ground rules.

There should be a door to the room where the workshop meets, and it should be kept closed if anyone else is at home. Adequate lighting and comfortable seats are important, too. Phones should never ring in the room, even when an answering machine picks up the calls; that rule includes cell phones and pagers, as well. Television sets and radios—even distant ones— should be silent, and children and dogs should be neither seen *nor* heard. Pets of any kind in the room (except maybe tropical fish) aren't a good idea. Someone once told me that there was a mynah bird in the room where her workshop met, and it had the habit of shrieking what sounded like editorial comments— "Good boy!" and "Uh-oh!"—during the critique of a manuscript, until its cage was covered.

Socializing between members must be reserved for the end of the meeting. Fiction writers, it seems to me, are particularly susceptible to the seductions of real life and of language in any form. Water may be provided during the meeting, but snacks are an annoying distraction. This is not a kaffeeklatsch; it's a serious professional meeting. Just think of how the crunch of potato chips would undermine the impact of a dramatic passage being read aloud, or how ineffective your earnest comments would be, offered through a mouthful of peanuts. I know of some groups that drink wine during their meetings, a practice they consider cosmopolitan and civilized, but I don't recommend it, any more than I'd recommend drinking alcohol while you write. Even a little buzz tends to blur one's judgment. (I always think that the drinking or pot-smoking writer who's ecstatic about his own work will have to get all his readers high, too.) And no matter how friendly and sympathetic you feel toward one another, the session should never disintegrate into a kind of group therapy. You're *not* there to unburden yourself or to resolve personal issues. A few people might want to go somewhere else afterward for coffee and conversation, and even the continuation of a critique, but this shouldn't be seen as an opportunity to gossip about absent workshop members or their work.

I've found that weekly meetings are ideal, with time out in the summer and during major holidays. Meeting more often than that usually puts too much pressure on some members, and meeting less often interrupts continuity. At the first session of a writing workshop, addresses (both E-mail and snail mail) and phone and fax numbers may be exchanged, and everyone should get to know everyone else, in a professional sense. The host-leader may ask each person to introduce himself, say a few words about his own writing and about the books he likes to read, and what he hopes to gain from being in a workshop. Even those who have been friends before will probably discover something new about one another. This is a good time to refer to published work (if any), previous workshops attended, and personal goals: "I want to finish a novel I've started"; "I hope to get published someday"; "I'd just like to improve this story I've written."

One's motives for writing, which are subtly different from one's realistic goals, are another interesting topic to explore. For instance, Flannery O'Connor said that she wrote because she was good at it. Dan Wakefield once confided—half seri-ously—that he did it to make the girls who wouldn't date him in high school sorry. Anne Tyler says she writes fiction because it gives her the chance to live additional lives. While Joan Didion maintains that we tell ourselves stories in order to live, Gloria Naylor admits that she hasn't a clue as to why she writes. I of-ten think that I write because I can't tap-dance, an early long-ing. But the most moving motivation I ever heard was expressed by Jackie Ruzas, an incarcerated writer, who said, "I write be-cause I can't fly."

The first impulse to write might derive from something as simple as wanting to please or displease someone else. As a child, I discovered that writing poems gleaned more positive at-tention from the grown-ups than anything else I did. If I got out of bed at night, using some lame excuse like needing another glass of water or another trip to the bathroom, I'd be sent right back to bed. But if I came into the kitchen and said that I'd just made up a poem, they'd stop talking or playing cards and let me recite it to them. So you could say that I really started writing to get attention. But the impetus to keep going usually comes from a more significant incentive, like having something urgent to say. Short-story writer Laura Foreman says, passionately and succinctly, that she writes because she *has* to. Examining our own motives—why did I write this particular story?—might help us to understand some problems with our work, especially if it seems trivial or petty at times.

Individual writing problems, like difficulty with plotting or characterization, may be *briefly* mentioned in those introductory workshop statements, but no one should go on too long or be too specific. It's up to the leader, using tact and firmness, to keep things moving. He might say, "We can talk more about that later, but we have to hear from everybody first." After everyone has had a chance to speak, the subject of format is introduced. The leader asks for suggestions from the group, and then, by a consensus, they decide how the workshop will be run. Here are some suggestions that come out of my own workshop experience.

Every member of the group should have a copy of each manuscript under discussion before the meeting. This is a simple matter of deciding who will present manuscripts the following week (or weeks), and then charging those writers with distributing copies of their work to everyone. Pages can be faxed to members or transmitted by E-mail. Using the old-fashioned method, manuscripts are handed out at the meeting the week before they're up for discussion. *They should be neatly typed and copied clearly.* This rule seems obvious, but in the past I've received blurry copies, illegibly handwritten submissions, and stories with other people's remarks scribbled all over them. *Page numbers* and *double spacing* make them easier to read, too, and *generous margins* allow room for notes and comments.

Everyone should read the manuscript in advance and make written, signed comments on it. I always write mine in pencil, to emphasize that they are only suggestions, not commandments. Written comments are invaluable to the writer. During the workshop, there's usually a barrage of oral response, both positive and negative, and it's often hard to absorb everything that's being said, and even harder to remember and sort it all out afterward. Signing your comments will help to keep them thoughtful and civil and give the recipient a chance to ask you for further explication later, if necessary. Even absentees should read the manuscripts and send written comments to the writer. You'll probably want to put a limit on the number of pages for submission, which can be frustrating to the more prolix writers among you. If you do have to select a section of a story or a part of a chapter that doesn't stand on its own, a brief written synopsis putting it in context is useful.

Anatole Broyard always had us read our work aloud to the group. He insisted that it was the ultimate test for a piece of prose. Listen for its music, he'd advise, or for those sour notes. If you keep stumbling over a word, that probably means you should chuck it. False or clumsy dialogue is especially noticeable when read aloud. Likewise, pretentious prose and too much exposition. Whenever it was my turn to read to the group, I'd find myself editing furiously as I went along, and I've heard people interrupt their own readings to say things like "Boy, this really stinks!"—something they hadn't noticed before in silent readings. Some shy writers suffer embarrassment during their workshop readings; one man in our group always had someone else read his story aloud for him, and he wore dark glasses while it was being read. (A recent survey determined that more people are afraid of public speaking than of death!) But all of us enjoyed the shared experience of being read to—just as we did as children—and the work was accordingly fresh in all of our minds.

Reading work aloud does take up a lot of the time that can be used for talking about it. Fewer manuscripts can be covered in a session if they're read aloud, and there is a certain amount of redundancy if everyone has already had a chance to read them himself. Work can also be made to sound better or worse than it actually is, according to the dramatic skills of the reader, making it difficult to render a valid opinion of it. A happy compromise, I believe, is to read short portions aloud in the workshop in order to demonstrate a critical point—that the dialogue is flat, for instance, or a description beautifully lyrical. But I still always read my own work aloud (to myself) after each draft.

The session's leader begins by designating which piece will be discussed first. This is usually an arbitrary choice, although a writer may request going first or last for personal reasons. Some people prefer to have their stories or novel chapters presented anonymously, out of modesty or fear, or because they believe they'll get a more impartial reading that way. But anonymity in a workshop reminds me of those guests on talk shows seen only in silhouette; I always wish I could see their eyes. Unless you're in a Federal Witness Protection Program, you should have the courage (the pride, actually) to be identified with your work. Fellow workshop members will probably start to recognize your fictional voice soon, anyway. And remember that professional, public criticism can be a lot harder to face, but would you ever choose to *publish* anonymously or use a pseudonym? I wouldn't.

If there's still time at the first meeting, after everyone's been properly introduced and all the ground rules have been set, somebody might present a short piece, no more than five or six pages, by reading it aloud. This serves as a little trial run of the workshop. At the first session of every group I've ever attended, at least one person brought a manuscript along, just in case. It takes a healthy mixture of vanity and guts to go first—to offer your work up to the mercy or cruelty of the group—but it's even harder to be the first to offer criticism. Right after the piece is read, there can be what seems like a damning silence, and a sudden inability for anyone to make eye contact with anyone else in the room. The children's game of "Statues" comes to mind, with everyone frozen in place. If that happens, the leader should ask for comments and, if they're not forthcoming, call on someone to speak or offer some remarks about the manuscript herself. That usually breaks the ice and other people will follow. The person speaking should be allowed to finish his remarks, unless they seem to go on forever or start to become repetitious. The leader should then gently interrupt and call on someone else. You don't have to follow anything as formal as parliamentary procedure; common courtesy and a sense of fairness are usually good enough, and spontaneity is very important. After the first session or two, discussion should flow more easily.

A few years ago, I visited a class of gifted fifth-graders in Columbia, South Carolina. The students had all written short memoirs or stories, which they were instructed to read aloud, followed by a response from their classmates. The teacher, an especially wise and sensitive woman, asked them to offer "comments" and "suggestions," a format they had obviously followed before. Their comments were mostly positive: "I loved it!" "I almost cried at the end," "I know *exactly* how you felt," and, even, "Your posture was really good," although a few were gently, tactfully negative: "I liked your last story more," "It was *sort* of funny," "There were so many big words." The suggestions tended to be more critical: "The mother was too mean," "You didn't put in enough about the boy's dog," and directly or indirectly encouraged revision. The praise they received first seemed to help those young writers withstand any ensuing disapproval of their work.

George Eliot wrote, "It is surely better to pardon too much than to condemn too much," and although I believe that most people learn more swiftly through positive conditioning, adults may not be so easily soothed by praise, especially in the early weeks of a workshop. As soon as the first negative response is uttered, the writer is inclined to come to his manuscript's defense—there's that courtroom metaphor again—but it's best for him to keep his counsel (no pun intended) until all the "evidence" is in. You just can't argue people out of their opinions or offer exculpatory material after the fact. *The manuscript must speak for itself.* Published books don't usually come with little notes tucked inside explaining the hero's hidden motives or that enigmatic passage on page 158. If your story is being discussed and you don't agree with some of the feedback, it doesn't help to say, defiantly, that your sister or your best friend was crazy about the piece just as it is. Remember that one of the reasons you joined the workshop was to receive informed, objective opinions from your peers, even if they do hurt a little. When something doesn't work for the reader, it might be because of some prejudice she holds, or a failure of her judgment or imagination, but it might also be due to a fault in the writing. It's good to listen to what everyone in the workshop has to say before concluding that the criticism is either flawed or accurate, and the leader should make sure that all the members have their say. As difficult as it may seem, the writer should hold his own response to the critique in abeyance until everyone else has spoken and he's called upon to respond by the leader, who may ask, "What do you think about what's been said?" By now I've heard every answer, from the perfunctory "Thanks a lot, everyone, that was really helpful" to "You idiots don't know what you're talking about!" The writer can also use his opportunity to speak, at last, to ask questions about concerns that weren't directly addressed by the others. "Nobody's mentioned the humor in the story. Did it work?" Or, "Was the point-of-view switch on page four too abrupt?" And he might ask for a clarification of any criticism he didn't understand.

Sometimes, it's hard to let go of the spotlight and that captive audience. Andy Warhol once said that in the future everyone would be world famous for fifteen minutes. I'm convinced that some people will always insist on at least twenty. The leader must keep track of the time and remember that there are other manuscripts waiting to be discussed. If the first critique and writer response go on too long, succeeding writers will be shortchanged. "I think that covers it," or "We really have to go on," is a reasonable way to curb the excess and keep things moving.

It's a good idea to take a quick break (no more than three to five minutes) between manuscripts. People will want to use the bathroom, or just get up and stretch. Everyone's mind will be restored by the pause—like a palate-cleansing sorbet served between courses—and ready to focus on the next piece of work.

Time may be reserved at the end of each meeting, or special meetings may be held, to talk more generally about writing and reading. This is a good opportunity to bring up larger craft issues, like moving from the short story to the novel, or to discuss philosophical aspects of writing fiction or to recommend books to one another. The second half of this book will deal with these useful discursions.

After a few sessions, inevitably you'll begin to find some members' criticism more valuable to you than others' or realize that you strongly favor someone's writing. You'll probably even like some *people* more than others. (I've made a few lifelong friends in workshops, myself.) This is only natural; the group is, after all, a microcosm of the external world, and a literary friendship can have extra dimension and depth. But the danger lies in forming exclusive little cliques that interfere with the collective camaraderie. And you will miss out if you stop listening to those who haven't been telling you what you want to hear. Remember that both writing skills *and* critical skills change and grow during the course of a workshop.

The true strength of an organized writing group lies in its cooperative nature, and mutual trust is a vital aspect of that cooperation. Members must know that what's said in the room will not be repeated elsewhere as dinner-party chitchat. And personal attacks are taboo; the *writing* is up for criticism, not the writer. It's quite easy—and awful—to be amusing at someone else's expense or to be condescending in our remarks. I've heard a few workshop tales that I believe and hope are apocryphal, like the one about the woman who announces in a dramatic whisper to her group that she's cursed; she's a writer. After she's read her story aloud, someone says, "I have good news for you. The curse has been lifted."

Everybody's work deserves a respectful and fair reading, even when it's not to the reader's liking, and it's important that everyone understands this from the beginning. As a teacher, I've had to deal with manuscripts that seemed to defy the possibility of constructive comment. One story was told completely from the viewpoint of a brain-dead man, and another opened with a woman choking (to death!) on her lover's condom. Believe it or not, serious, useful criticism—related to credibility, sympathy, etc.—was offered by the group about both these stories. The same critical standards must be applied to *all* manuscripts. These standards will be discussed in the next chapter, on reading and criticism.

A workshop is not a contest. There will not be a winner, or any losers, for that matter, at the end of each session. The only competition should be between the previous version of your manuscript and the revised one. You will want to make it better, or as Grace Paley advises, "truer."

After several sessions, a kind of natural rhythm starts to set in at most workshops, and you may decide to dispense with even the informal, rotating "leadership." The force of habit and a growing respect for one another should keep things moving smoothly.

3

Read, Mark, Learn

'Tis the good reader that makes the good book.

—RALPH WALDO EMERSON

Many of us can vividly recall a particular passage in a favorite book, even one that was read a long time ago, though our recollection of recent personal events may be pretty fuzzy. This usually says more about the indelibility of good fiction than it does about short-term memory loss. Avid readers speak of "losing" themselves in a fictional narrative, of coming back to reality like sleepers awakened rudely from a dream. But the novelist Stanley Elkin wrote, "[The act of reading] is not so much a way of forgetting ourselves as of engaging the totality of our attentions, as racing car drivers or mountain climbers engage them, as surgeons and chess masters do." He might have included writers in his list, as well. The ability of the writer to focus so intently on his fictional world is probably learned from his experience as a reader. I'd even go so far as to say that a love of reading invariably precedes the desire to write. Yet many new writers admit, even brag, that they don't read very much. They claim to be "natural" writers, who are self-educated in something like the "University of Life." I agree that there is such a thing as inborn talent, and of course all experience is useful to a writer, but other people's books are an intrinsic part of that experience, and I don't trust a writer's education that doesn't include a lot of reading. How can he be sure that what he believes he's just invented wasn't thought up by other, earlier writers, and how will he build, as we all must, on their discoveries and insights?

I can still remember first learning to read, using the phonic method and my index finger to track the daily doings of Dick and Jane and Spot. They were pretty dull characters, but they led me into the kingdom of reading, and their predictable little stories only whet my appetite for better ones. I grew up in a crowded three-generation household that didn't have many books but was rife with good stories, usually related in the kitchen, where I loitered, under the blue enamel table, just so I might overhear them. My family spoke three languages at home—English, Yiddish, and pig Latin—and I listened to the serialized tale of their lives, told through reminiscences, gossip, complaints, and jokes, in that delicious mix of tongues, until someone noticed I was there and warned, "Ix-nay, the id-kay!" No wonder Flannery O'Connor said that "anybody who has survived his childhood has enough information about life to last him the rest of his days." Those tender, green days of life, during which you receive your first impressions of love and death, have a profound and lasting effect on your adult sense of self and others. The child who goes to bed early is thrillingly aware of those allowed to stay up late. An early habit of eavesdropping is not uncommon among writers. In Eudora Welty's memoir, *One Writer's Beginnings*, she writes: "Long before I wrote stories, I listened for stories. Listening *for* them is something more acute than listening *to* them."

But after I realized that the juiciest parts of my family's oral narratives were being censored, I went in search of a good *written* narrative. I began to read everything in sight, from the back of the cereal box to the magnified directions on the label inside the shampoo bottle. My parents' scant library included, mysteriously, just the illustrated *cover* to an edition of *Huckleberry Finn*; an ancient set of encyclopedias called *The Book of Knowledge*, which I proceeded to go through alphabetically; *Hitty: Her First Hundred Years*, a children's book about a doll; and a heavy tome called *Dr. Morris Fischbein's Home Medical Adviser*, with a long catalogue of fascinating and gruesome symptoms. I think I became a hypochondriac long before I became a writer!

Eventually, I found a book that drew me in by the sheer power of its language. It was *Penrod* by Booth Tarkington. Its very first sentence—"Penrod sat morosely upon the back fence and gazed with envy at Duke, his wistful dog"—contained at least two words I'd never encountered before: "morosely" and "wistful." (As the middle child in the family, I probably knew intuitively about envy.) The illustration of Penrod and Duke right above that first sentence gave me a clue to its meaning, and I must have asked my mother about it, as well. But I remember sounding those two unknown words out first, hearing their sibilant music and almost tasting their foreign flavor in my mouth. That, I believe, was the beginning of a love affair with reading that ultimately led to my becoming a writer. Along the way, I also picked up a few critical skills. I began to notice that some books were condescending to children in their language and tone, or overwritten, depriving me of the reader's work of imagining. There were writers whose characters all seemed alike, or unlike anyone at all, and books without any moral complexity or suspense. Of course there were also the dazzling works of Dickens and Twain and the Brontës. Finding a story that seems fresh and familiar at once, with believable, memorable characters and a solid plot, still excites me.

A reasonable law is that good readers make better critics, and better critics make better writers. Most of us don't read in order to become better critics, though; we read for a variety of other reasons—to be informed, to be entertained, to gain insight, and to be consoled, among them. Reading for pleasure is one thing and reading critically quite another, and much more like work. So I'll often pick up a student's or friend's manuscript as if I were opening the pages of a published novel, with the happy anticipation of being transported, of being drawn into someone else's fictional dream. After the first read through, I'll start all over again, this time with a colder, more incisive eye, and with my pencil in hand.

My initial reaction to anything I read is usually visceral and personal, very much like those fifth-grade kids in South Carolina. I really like this! I hate it! It's hilarious! It makes me feel so sad! If I don't think or feel *anything*, that's pretty damning. In a letter to a writer friend, Paul Bowles wrote, "Don't you want readers to be disturbed? I wrote *hoping* they'd find the material wayward enough to be upsetting." Every fiction writer hopes to elicit an intellectual and/or emotional response from the reader. The failure to do so or the failure to evoke that willing suspension of disbelief may be seen as a *failure of intention*. Therefore the first question that comes to mind when I'm reading as a workshop teacher/critic is, What did the writer intend? This is a good way to start off a discussion, too. The success of the manuscript depends on the fulfillment of this objective, although occasionally the writer discovers his own unconscious intentions only after the work is written: so *this* is what I wanted to say! Sometimes I can't discern any intention at all in an unsatisfactory manuscript, and in the margin I might ask, "What's this story trying to say?" A new writer may be offended by the question. *He* understands the story perfectly; if I don't get it, it must be *my* problem. But if a majority of readers don't get it, it could be the writer's problem. Perhaps, in a desire not to be obvious or expository, he's left a lot of the narrative in his head. Or perhaps he's not so sure of his intentions, either. I used to write, "What's this story about?" but that was sometimes misunderstood. A few people thought I meant that the story or its developing plot wasn't clear, when I was actually referring to the theme, the underlying imperative for writing the story. In *Aspects of the Novel*, E. M. Forster writes, " 'The king died and then the queen died,' is a story. 'The king died, and then the queen died of grief' is a plot." The theme, in that case, would be the tragedy of love and loss. And if the reader doesn't get *that*, I'm afraid everything else will be lost.

Here are some other general questions I'll ask myself when evaluating a student's or colleague's work, and they should help you frame your workshop discussions.

Do I Believe This Story?

Belief in a story doesn't imply that I think it's based on fact—perhaps the writer's own experience—and that I'm looking for the real lowdown. As it happens, fiction prompted by real life is often hampered by the writer's inability to deviate from the actual events that inspired her, whether by rearranging those events or just making things up. She should be reminded that even memoirs presented as pure truth are subject to the vagaries of memory. Why else would two children in the same family recall conflicting versions of a single event? The poorest, and most commonly heard, defense of unpersuasive fiction is that it really happened. Who cares? We can "believe" a work of pure fantasy because it presents certain intrinsic truths about the way we live and relate to one another. We all know that little red-hooded girls and their grandmothers are not gobbled up by wolves only to be rescued later—intact!—by dashing huntsmen. But beyond that dubious story line, there are the recognizable truths of familial affection and of greed, innocence (and its loss), mortal danger, and acts of heroism. In Gabriel García Márquez's brilliant novel *One Hundred Years of Solitude*, the narrator's father "discovers" ice in a mythical Latin American town, and we momentarily suspend our disbelief to accept this event of pure magic realism. When E. L. Doctorow intermingles actual historical figures with invented characters in *Ragtime*, we don't object to his novelistic revision of history. (An editor once asked him if J. P. Morgan and Henry Ford had actually met, and Doctorow replied, "They have now.") And when we read a Vietnam War novel by Tim O'Brien or Robert Olen Butler, it's important not that we actually *know* that both writers served in Vietnam, but that they have made that place and that war intensely real for us through their writing. My own first novel, *Ending*, was about a young husband and father's death from cancer, something I'd imagined, but fortunately hadn't experienced. After a public reading I gave, an elderly woman came up to me, gently patted my arm and said, with great sympathy,

"How long have you been widowed, dear?" Of course I was delighted that she had found my fiction so convincing, although my husband, who was standing right next to me at the time, was not.

Our intense curiosity about the private lives of writers is a modern phenomenon fostered by advanced technology. It used to be enough simply to believe in the life disclosed between the covers of the book, and to know that a favorite writer was still alive somewhere and might deliver a sequel one day. Now we want to know, and often get the chance to ask, whether he's married, if he writes in the morning or the afternoon, and where he gets his ideas. Imagine Flaubert appearing on "Larry King Live" to confess: *"Madame Bovary, c'est moi!"* Personally, I'd rather read the book. In a workshop, the writer is right there, in the flesh, but it's important to look at his story without employing your knowledge or curiosity about his private life. Allow the writer to become invisible, so that only his work is up for contemplation and discussion. The "truth" of a manuscript lies in the reader's unconditional acceptance of it.

One important afterthought about establishing credibility: Although the gutsy and gifted writer might deliberately embellish or reinvent history, as García Márquez and Doctorow do, or create a surreal dream landscape, like Lewis Carroll's Wonderland and L. Frank Baum's Oz, without sacrificing the reader's faith in his story, *unintentional* mistakes of fact can be deadly. A friend who was an enthusiastic fan of a popular and prolific novelist abruptly stopped reading him after discovering, in one of his novels, that a character drives across the Manhattan Bridge into New Jersey! "I just couldn't trust him again after that," my friend said sadly. I was spared—by an early, alert reader of one of my manuscripts—the embarrassment of setting key scenes in the basement of a house in Levittown, Long Island, where, in fact, there are no basements. Which only proves that a little research (and a lot of emotional truth) can go a long way toward gaining the reader's trust.

Do I Care About the Characters?

I've always believed that the best fiction is character driven. Where would novels like *Jane Eyre* and *Little Women* be without their larger-than-life heroines? John Updike once wrote critically of J. D. Salinger that he loves his characters more than God does, but I've never considered that a capital offense. If we don't love them, who will? But can I really care about E. M. Forster's king and queen, or any of Shakespeare's suffering sovereigns, for that matter? King *who?* I don't happen to know any royalty, myself, and even a story of love and loss won't really move me unless I can empathize with the people who are experiencing them. The writer's greatest challenge is to make his characters and their plight idiosyncratic—"everyman" isn't very compelling—yet universally recognizable. I might be drawn into a tale about kings and queens precisely *because* their lives are so different from mine (reading for information and entertainment), but I'll stay with it only if I can relate to the characters and their circumstances, if they somehow reflect my own inner life (reading for insight and consolation). Kings and queens are, finally, only human.

Some of my favorite characters in fiction are male (Penrod, of course, Holden Caulfield in Salinger's *The Catcher in the Rye*, Douglas Bridge in Evan S. Connell's *Mrs. Bridge* and *Mr. Bridge*, and Nathanael West's eponymous Miss Lonelyhearts); or from another country and century (Scheherazade, the enterprising heroine of the *Arabian Nights*, and Elizabeth Bennet in Jane

Austen's *Pride and Prejudice*); or from a different species (Charlotte and Wilbur in E. B. White's *Charlotte's Web,* and any of the unanthropomorphized dogs in Ann Beattie's and Anne Tyler's novels). These various characters stay in my mind for a number of reasons that include their complexity, courage, intelligence, off-beat charm, humor, pathos, or style. In certain respects, they're all foreign to my own experience, yet in each one I encounter the particular joy of recognition.

Is the Voice Convincing and Compelling?

This is a tricky, but not really a trick, question. First we must try to define what we mean by fictional voice. John Fowles says that it's "the overall impression one has of the creator behind what he creates," which brings me back to Oz. In our fictional kingdoms, each of us is the wizard, the mysterious voice behind the screen. This doesn't mean that we must limit ourselves to our own experience and sensibility, even when we're using the first person. We're writers, not ventriloquists. A young male novelist using the "I" voice of an elderly Southern woman living in the middle of the twentieth century should employ an inflection and tone that recall the time and place of the story, yet also reflect his heroine's particular personality, and even something of her personal history, like the extent of her education and worldly experience. Read Allan Gurganus's *Oldest Living Confederate Widow Tells All* for the consummate example of a character revealed by her own voice, which also offers a distinct impression of her creator.

The first time I attempted to write in the first-person voice of a male character—a thirteen-year-old boy named Bernie—my editor, Michael di Capua, said he liked the story, with one major reservation: Bernie sounded an awful lot like a fifty-year-old woman. Voice was clearly the problem, and it took about a year and a complete rewrite to remedy it. During that time, I listened to teenage boys talking on the subways and in the streets, paying particular attention to their vocabulary and diction. But overloading my protagonist's narrative with such common teen phrases as "I'm, like, really freaking" and "Cool, man" made it seem even less authentic (fifty-year-old woman doing *impression* of thirteen-year-old boy). Reading the work aloud as I revised really helped. That's how I discovered that a contemporary kid who's run away from home is unlikely to recollect, "On the day of my departure . . ." And *I* might say I was getting groggy; Bernie would be more apt to feel "spacey" or "zonked." My "nagging" had to become his "bugging," and so on.

In a series of letters to di Capua during the overhaul of the manuscript, I wrote the following:

"After about seven new drafts, this one woke me in the middle of the night. I hope it's a true voice trying to speak to me. . . . I've become very conscious of Bernie's voice, his way of seeing things and his language. He now refers to Nat [his mother's boyfriend] as 'this guy she's going out with' rather than as 'a widower'. . . . The good thing is that I'm starting to *enjoy* revising, and to like the book for better reasons, I think—less out of vanity and pride than because of my connection to the characters. . . ." I worked hard at keeping Bernie's voice consistent without becoming one-note. Still, I didn't feel satisfied until a teenage boy working in the publisher's mailroom read the revised manuscript and declared my narrator believably male and young.

But in a narrative related in the third person, whose voice are we talking about? God's? The author's? The central character's? The answer is different for different books, and might be any of the three or a composite of two or all of them. In the southern milieu again, I think of Flannery O'Connor, whose faith certainly informed her stories—allowing even the sorriest character a kind of redemption—yet who never sounds didactic or pontifical. Instead, she's wryly funny and truly egalitarian, letting her characters speak for themselves, and for her, in marvelously eccentric ways. Who can ever forget the Misfit, the highway assassin in "A Good Man Is Hard to Find"? After shooting a particularly garrulous old lady to death, he remarks, "She would of been a good woman if it had been someone there to shoot her every minute of her life."

That line demonstrates that fictional voice is much more than just a matter of using the first or third person. Joyce Carol Oates refers to its "indefinable/unmistakable beat." Some of its other subtle components include tone, diction, inflection, and attitude, plus a few intangibles—what we might define collectively as "personality" in someone we know. The trust that the reader places in the writer is violated when a character commits verbal anachronisms ("Gimme a break!" in an eighteenth-century setting, or "Forsooth, varlet," in the twenty-first; when the voice just isn't in synch with the story or the character's disposition; or when the point of view seems to be unreliable or vague. Such blunders can be jarring and even fatal to the reader's engagement with the work.

Does the Story Have Narrative and Emotional Suspense?

Narrative and emotional suspense are two separate yet interconnected considerations. The bedtime stories we once listened to over and over again, until we knew them by heart, still had a kind of renewable suspense, as if they might have miraculously changed between tellings. Does Goldilocks get away safely from the bears *this* time? Will the prince still try the glass slipper on that raggedy girl sitting among the cinders, and will it fit? That's narrative suspense in its purest form, the element that inspires the reader to turn the pages. But sometimes a writer foreshadows upcoming events too heavily or simply announces what happens (telling, not showing), flattening the reader's thrill of discovery. Whenever we sense authorial manipulation, the story's impact is diminished.

The same is true of emotional suspense. To achieve it, *the writer should never tell the reader how to feel.* That can only come from our connection to the characters and our curiosity about them. What are their interior lives like, and are we caught up in them? And what psychological changes occur as a consequence of their actions? Has Goldilocks learned a lesson about straying too far from home? Will her independent spirit be quashed in the process? Will Cinderella and her prince really live happily ever after, and will she ever forgive her rotten stepmother and stepsisters? A story that doesn't arouse these concerns—that doesn't make the reader project the characters into their unknown future—may be a lively read, but it won't have any lasting resonance. When a child writes to ask what happens to a character *after* the end of the book, I always take it as a great compliment.

On occasion the narrative suspense of a story is sacrificed—successfully—to its emotional suspense, by the use of the flashback. In Alice McDermott's novel *Charming Billy*, we learn right up front that Billy Lynch has died of alcoholism and that his entire life was blighted by a lie told to him about a lost love. What makes the reader eager to read on is the retrospective unfolding of these foretold events, her desire to see them happen, through Billy's eyes. And Judith Rossner's best-selling *Looking for Mr. Goodbar* opens with the arrest of a man for the murder of the book's heroine. Hardly a whodunit, but wonderfully suspenseful anyway.

Is the Tense Right?

During the seventies and eighties, there appeared a plethora of stories told in the present tense. Lynne Sharon Schwartz equated this literary outbreak with an epidemic of flu. "But while influenza does its worst to old people," she wrote, "the present tense for the most part strikes at the young." Almost immediately, critical camps arose, both for and against its usage. The main argument for the present tense is that it creates a sense of immediacy and urgency, of someone whispering in your ear about events that are happening at that very moment. I applied it in one novel, myself, for just that purpose. But the present tense can seem precious and affected after a while, as I began to suspect it was in my manuscript. I also noticed that my characters suffered from a decided lack of reflection and analysis, as they lived only in and for the moment. I was able to ameliorate these problems somewhat by switching to the past tense (with its historical tone) for retrospective scenes.

The past perfect tense—"He'd had a terrible time learning the language"—may be established at the beginning of a paragraph and then dropped in the succeeding sentence: "He mispronounced almost everything," without disorienting the reader. I don't hold with any hard-and-fast rules about tense except that, like voice, it must suit the story being told. Again, reading the work aloud will help you and your workshop members to see if you've made the right choices.

Where Is the Ache in This Story?

This is a question cribbed directly from Anatole Broyard, who asked it whenever he surmised that one of us in his workshop had written a story from a pure, coldly intellectual impulse. In his view, such a story was missing an important component, which he chose to call "the ache." He was not looking for *sentimentality*, which he abhorred, but for the more honestly felt and less manipulative quality of *sentiment*. You could admire a story without an ache, he said, but you might not enjoy it in a deep and enduring way. Our characters had to *want* something, Broyard told us, and we had to address their desires, whether or not we fulfilled them.

I was once on a panel to judge submissions to a writing contest. One of my copanelists, James Alan McPherson, and I were the lone supporters of an obviously flawed story that had what he referred to as "heart." I knew what he meant. We were both moved and persuaded by the story, which, admittedly, might have been tighter and written more elegantly, as were some of the other, more popular finalists. We didn't prevail in the contest, but I still remember the entry that lost and the emotional effect it had on me. To achieve true sentiment, or heart, or that ache—whatever you want to call it—you may have to risk being maudlin. Salinger and Dickens took the chance and succeeded; many others have failed. I still think it's worth the gamble.

Would I Continue Reading This If I Didn't Have To?

This may be the most telling question asked about any piece of writing. Although we often revisit the classics, read contemporary books recommended by friends or professional critics, or read books by authors whose previous works we've liked, we also browse in libraries and bookstores, picking up an unknown book and reading partway into it to see if we're drawn in by the story and the way it's told. If not, we can always put it down and start reading something else. Unfortunately, there's an obligation to keep reading a fellow workshop member's manuscript, even when it doesn't suit your taste, even when it's badly written or downright boring. That's what you're there for: to pinpoint what doesn't work and—as significantly—what does. And of course the same courtesy will be extended to you. But it's fair to comment that although you read the whole manuscript, you didn't feel *compelled* to do so, for one reason or another: it was too wordy, too slow, too static, the characters didn't engage or convince you, and so on.

Is the Language Well Chosen?

After all the larger issues of intention, character, suspense, and the like are addressed, attention must be paid to the minute details of language. Proust's madeleine may have been made with sugar and flour and butter and eggs, but his novels (and ours) are composed only of words. I was once advised to think of words as "expensive" and of myself as being on a tight budget. It was an admonition to choose carefully, to make sure that every word I used mattered and was the best possible one for its purpose. Sometimes words in a manuscript are inaccurate; the writer means to say "respective" but writes "respectful," or mistakes "scarifying" for "scary." At other times the word choice is merely inexact: "happiness" instead of the more exultant "glee," the overstatement of "distraught" when "upset" would have been enough. What sets fresh and talented writing apart from triter efforts is often the selection of individual words or phrases. In Lorrie Moore's story "Terrific Mother," a wife places her hand on her husband's chest "like a medallion, like a necklace of sleep." How strange and beautiful and *right* that sounds!

And if you think there's not much difference between such familiar and seemingly inconsequential words as "yes," and "yeah," imagine Molly Bloom in her soliloquy crying, "And yeah, I said. Yeah, okay, I will, sure, right." Or the Beatles singing, "She loves you, yep, yep, yep." When Cormac McCarthy's South-westerners substitute "kindly" for "kind of" and Grace Paley's irrepressible New Yorkers use expressions like "I'm dying on my dogs" and "Don't take any woolen condoms," the reader is immediately grounded in place and character. All words, of course, must be read in the context of their sentences and the sentences within their paragraphs.

The most significant change I ever made in a manuscript involved a single word, or more precisely, a single *letter*. It was in my novel *Ending*, mentioned above. When the husband dies, a nurse informs his wife of the death by saying, "He's gone," and the wife is disturbed by the euphemism. In an early version of that chapter, she looks at her husband's dead body and thinks: "The nurse was right. Gone was the right word after all. The force of life, gone. The miracle of motion, gone. Nothing." Ted Solotaroff, the astute editor who'd pressed for other, more substantial changes throughout the manuscript, made only one tiny mark on this page, simply adding the letter *e* at the beginning of the word *motion*, so that the sentence now read: "The miracle of emotion, gone." Hardly a major rewrite, but what a difference in meaning it achieved!

This sort of invaluable scrutiny is multiplied in the workshop. It's like having *several* editors examining the work at once, and what one person might not notice, another is likely to.

The marked-up workshop manuscript usually highlights individual words that don't work for the reader. When something is a cliché, the note could say just that or "Something fresher here?" or "familiar." When the word in question is simply not right, "imprecise" or "off" will convey that. Any words that jump out of a sentence, announcing themselves, what one student aptly called the "showoffs," could be noted as "jarring" or "out of voice." In the same context, Faulkner advised: "We must kill our darlings." It's tempting for the reader-critic to replace an offending word with something she thinks is better. *Suggestions* are certainly OK, but I believe it's the writer's job (and privilege) to rewrite her own manuscript.

The members of your workshop are likely to come up with other questions and concerns about individual manuscripts. Your comments, written and spoken, should always be framed in a way that will help guide the writer to an improved version of her work.

4

Subject to Change

INTERVIEWER: "How many drafts of a story do you do?"
S. J. PERELMAN: "Thirty-seven. I once tried doing thirty-three, but something was lacking, a certain—how shall I say—je ne sais quoi. On another occasion, I tried forty-two versions, but the final effect was too lapidary. . . ."

—*WRITERS AT WORK:*
THE PARIS REVIEW INTERVIEWS

Interviews with established writers can be useful reading for workshop members, who are naturally curious about those work habits that contribute to success. A marked-up manuscript page precedes each of the *Paris Review* interviews, and they reveal as much about the creative process as what the writers themselves have to say about their craft. It's enlightening to see one word deleted in favor of another—Irwin Shaw choosing the specificity of "February" over the more general "winter," Hemingway replacing "Yeah" with "Sure"—or an entire passage simply stricken from the page. And it's encouraging to realize that even seasoned novelists and poets rigorously revise, that no literary work pops out in absolutely perfect, final form from anyone's head.

You'll notice that some of the accompanying manuscript pages are handwritten and others typed on various kinds of machines. Famous writers are often asked on public occasions if they use a computer or a pen. The more sophisticated members of the audience groan in embarrassment at the naïveté of the question—as if mere mechanics will reveal the secret to anyone's success! But, like magicians, we all look for the sleight of hand that will fool not only our audience but ourselves. In the process, each of us develops particular rituals that get us going, that keep us going. These rituals are essential, even sacred, but of course it's not the method that counts so much as the creative madness that impels it. When Bernard Malamud said that the thing was to get that pencil moving every morning, it was the movement, not the pencil, that really mattered. Yet it's intriguing to imagine Hemingway standing at a kind of bookcase-lectern writing with his pencil, one of twenty he's said to have sharpened every morning; to learn that Robert Frost would write almost anywhere except at a desk, even on the sole of his shoe; and that Georges Simenon once expressed a desire to carve a novel into a piece of wood. And it can be quite useful to examine other writers' techniques of revision.

When I'm writing I jot down some notes by hand, especially if I'm not at my regular workstation, and when I remember I carry some paper or a notepad for that purpose. But when I forget, I'm forced to decipher lines I've scribbled in my checkbook or in the margins of the newspaper. That is, if I haven't thrown the newspaper out (a more efficient friend writes on her own wrist). I'm not sure why, but inspiration often strikes at the least convenient times and places—in the middle of the night, for instance, or when I'm jogging, driving, or taking a shower. Someone once gave me some soap crayons for the shower walls, but I felt as if I were scrawling graffiti in my own bathroom (STOP ME BEFORE I WRITE AGAIN!), and my words were often rinsed away by mistake. A small tape recorder might have come in handier. I usually write directly onto the computer, but I always print my work out at the end of each day, or even more often than that. Somehow it's easier to read critically from hard copy—which you can conveniently take with you on the bus or into the bathtub—and to revise in its margins. When my marked-up pages come to resemble flypaper in a deli, I'll enter the changes on the computer. Here's a sample page of the second draft of an old, eventually abandoned short story before it was retyped. As you can see (if you can read my handwriting; those large, even margins I'm always recommending would have helped), I had several second thoughts, most of them involving *additions* to the manuscript. Before I committed myself to writing, I dabbled for a little while in sculpture. In the first class I took, at the Brooklyn Museum of Art School, we were each given a piece of soapstone and a couple of chisels. A model sat before us on a platform, and we were expected to reproduce her image in our chunks of stone. Unlike Michelangelo, who was said to liberate his figures from their marble prisons, I just kept chipping away with my chisels until I had nothing before me but a pile of soapstone dust. This was pretty discouraging, but I persisted. I even signed up for another class, in which we worked in clay, building outward from a small wire armature. For some reason I was able to make some reasonable replicas of the model that way. Accordingly, there are two kinds of writers: the chippers, who tend to overwrite and must chip away their excesses when they workers talk that way, as if there's a vocabulary test they have to take before they get their license. With words like "constructive" and"life goals" and"obsession" on it. They all sound the same after a while.

I was looking for my mother, but I was doing other things, too. If a person is obsessed, she can only do that one thing. If she's crazy she can't tell what's real and what is imagined.

A few weeks ago a woman was on one of the shows telling about her twenty-year search for her real mother and father. I couldn't believe it. It was one of those long complicated stories and the woman kept breaking down and crying, and the interviewer made little soothing noises, but you could see he was happy because it made the show better. He said, "Uh-huh," and "This must be very difficult for you," and "these are tears of joy," etc. etc.

Everything in the world had happened to that woman. She was separated from her parents in a concentration camp during world war II. For years each thought the others were dead. When she was still a kid she was brought to America by an agency and adopted by a couple who then split up. The wife kept the child and then the husband kidnapped her and took her to South America. You name it and it had happened to that woman. Of course she finally found her real mother--the Nazis had killed her father just before the camp was liberated. Her mother came out on a revolving stage and she was an old, old woman with glasses so thick you couldn't see her eyes, and a big ugly corsage that practically pulled her dress off her shoulder. Everyone applauded and people cried and the sponsor gave her them a get-acquainted trip to Mexico City and Acapulco. I couldn't imagine why they'd want to travel anywhere ever again.

revise; and the builders (like me) who usually end up adding words and texture to the spare framework of a story. In the workshop, we gradually come to recognize each other's writing methods and to respect them. I have to be careful that I don't impose my own preference for economy on those whose style is naturally more baroque; less isn't necessarily more for everybody. As a colleague once complained, "You're reducing my four-generation saga to haiku!"

Some of my revisions on this sample page may seem fussy and picayune. Does it really matter if you say "too" or "besides," if the stage is "dark" or "darkened?" Well, yes. "Besides" may be more native to someone's vocabulary than "too," and I think it sounds more defensive, which my character is. "Dark" seems absolute; "darkened" allows for some play of light and shadow, for a certain amount of visibility. Accuracy is essential, and *every word counts,* even when the effect of small changes is only cumulative.

Larger, structural changes make a more dramatic and conspicuous impact on the work. Often, blocks of prose can be moved (with some adjustments) from one part of a manuscript to another—the old cut-and-paste routine. And sometimes it takes an outside reader, like one of your workshop members, to see how to do this. A workshop friend named Elaine Greene, who'd read a late draft of my second novel, *In the Flesh*, suggested just such a change. The book is about a young New York City couple whose marriage survives infidelity and other stresses and strains. They stay together for a number of reasons, including habit and the children, but mainly because of their battered yet enduring love for one another. They decide to find neutral ground on which to begin anew, so they leave their beloved city and move to the suburbs. The version of the manuscript that Elaine read ended, in keeping with its chronological order, with the family living in their new house.

> *I took a walk with the children in that profound absence of traffic and other walkers. The lawn sprinklers moved back and forth with the precision of Rockettes. Women on their lawns and porches were friendly. When they saw me with Jason and Ann, who fit nicely into the mean age of all the children in the neighborhood, they waved and invited us to visit. It was spring in the suburbs, as it was in the city, but out there it announced itself in full orchestra. During my walk I felt that I would probably be able to forgive Howard, that we could clean the whole slate and start all over again. It might take a while, I knew, but I believed we could do it. What I would have trouble dealing with was the heartbreaking leafiness of all those trees and the earth-sprung shoots of grass underfoot. What I probably couldn't ever forgive was the joyous riot of birdsong wherever I went.*

Elaine suggested that the following, *earlier* passage, recording the family's move from the city—where most of the novel takes place—would make a more poignant and meaningful ending.

> *The moving men were like Chinese acrobats I had once seen in a circus; squat and powerful and communicating in wordless grunts. They worked perfectly in teams, our furniture on their backs, until the rooms were completely bare. I went on a brief tour of inspection. A rusted steel wool pad on the kitchen counter, a collapsed pacifier in the dust where the baby's crib had been, and, in the*

shower stall, delicate curls of pubic hair, gender unknown.
  Howard, always mindful of ceremony, came upstairs
again with the children in his arms, and we all took one
last look together. The baby, because she was hungry or
tired, or from some deep, intuitive knowledge, began to
cry, and we left quickly, leaving the door open, and we
didn't look back.

I realized that Elaine (who happens to be an experienced editor) was right; the latter passage *did* make a stronger and more relevant ending. The symbolism of the empty rooms, with their scattered domestic artifacts, was truer about this couple's past and more prophetic about their future than the cheery suburban references to rebirth and renewal. But I still liked the other paragraph, too, and I wanted to keep it in the novel without disturbing the chronology of events. So I juggled things—the suburban walk now takes place *before* the move, on a visit to inspect the house while it's being painted—and I switched the two passages. I also wrote some new material to make the transition from one passage to the other smoother. Of course I had to reread *everything* in its revised context, to be sure that it made sense and appeared seamless. Since then I've often moved passages, even whole chapters, from one place to another. It helps to think of the manuscript as a deck of cards that can be reshuffled and laid out in many different ways, in order to achieve a better "hand."

A first draft (of a story or a chapter, at least) may be written in a single passionate session, without subsequent alterations in mind. Raymond Carver and Tess Gallagher, who were husband and wife, worked closely together on revisions of their respective stories. She says that he always advised her to "write that draft as quickly as possible, not lifting my pen from the page, getting the swoop and lift of the story down as one motion. Later, details could be sharpened and amplified. Corrections of language and timing could be made."

But there are writers who have trouble changing a single word in their work at any time, even when they recognize that it might be improved. They view their stories as delicate structures that might disintegrate under the weight of revision. Yet revision is a natural part of our daily lives. In restaurants we change our order and have the lasagna instead of the halibut; in our cars we switch on a whim from the shortcut to the scenic route; we even decide to marry Tom after being engaged to Dick or Harry for a while. Hemlines go up and down. Moves are made from the country to the city and then back again. The ability to choose and the flexibility to change our minds make our lives better and freer. Adjustments can be liberating in our writing as well.

Over the years, I've seen several impressive transformations take place in workshops. A writer who couldn't seem to put his metaphorical finger on the problem with a story had a sudden breakthrough because of the criticism of someone *else's* work. And a group member whose writing didn't seem all that promising made an unexpected and daring leap in his work, inspired by a casual suggestion from one of his peers. I like to think of this happy phenomenon as a "laying on" of words. When I was teaching in the graduate writing program at the University of Iowa, I also led a fiction workshop of undergraduates, most of them freshmen. These recent high school students had very little writing experience beyond assigned book reports, topical essays, and the autobiographical sketches they'd done for freshman comp. Many of them had only read books they absolutely had to, and their worldly experience was pretty limited, too. It wasn't surprising to find that the manuscripts they'd turned in for the workshop tended to be both sophomoric and solipsistic. What did surprise me was the ability of some of these students to listen intelligently to criticism and then use it to good advantage.

One young man—we'll call him Kevin—wrote a thinly veiled "story" about his own recent departure from the state of Washington and the girlfriend he'd reluctantly left behind. One passage read, "Allison was standing at the sink doing the dishes. 'Good-bye,' I said, and my eyes filled with tears." When I asked for a class response, someone said we might become more involved in the story if we had some idea of how Allison looked when they were saying good-bye. The following week, Kevin dutifully turned in a revised manuscript. The criticized passage now read, "Allison was standing at the sink doing the dishes. She's five ten with long blond hair and blue eyes and she looks like a model. 'Good-bye,' I said, and my eyes filled with tears." I explained to Kevin that we didn't want her statistics or a description that read more like a cop's make on a criminal. What might help us feel the protagonist's pain at leaving Allison would be her *essence,* whatever it is that makes him love her. *He* knows what she looks like, I said, but he has to convey that to us without being too expository, and without bringing the story to a screeching halt while he does so. That was Kevin's writing assignment for the next class. The following week, he showed up with a third draft. This time the passage under discussion read, "Allison was standing at the sink doing the dishes. Her long blond hair was pinned up, so that her neck and just the tips of her ears were exposed. 'Good-bye,' I said, and my eyes filled with tears." Mine did, too! I felt as pleased and proud as

Professor Higgins when Eliza Doolittle finally perfects her diction.

In a workshop at the Bread Loaf Writers' Conference, the simple excision of an extravagant number of adjectives from someone's story, at the suggestion of another participant, revealed some very nice unadorned prose, proving that less often *is* more. The critic hadn't imposed her own rewrite on the story; she'd merely stripped away the writer's excesses, and voilà!— there were the bare bones of a good story. A similar effect occurred when someone else removed a bunch of adverbs, which tend to tell rather than show, anyway, and are often redundant. What a character chooses to say or do is usually enough to convey his mood and motivations. " 'Damn it to hell!' he shouted angrily, banging his fist on the table," is definitely overkill. So is a "Tom Swifty" like, " 'I'm truly *sorry*,' she said *contritely*." On another occasion at Bread Loaf, a man was surprised to discover that he'd used a number of marine-related similes in his story: "He floundered around"; " 'Stop carping,' she said"; " 'There's something fishy going on around here' "; "Waves of nausea assaulted him," and so on. All of us eventually fall prey to some sort of writing tic. One of mine is the overuse of certain simple, relatively inconspicuous words, such as *look*, or *just*. My editor might return a single page of a manuscript with the same word circled ten or fifteen times. Although "look" can have different meanings in different instances—" 'Look here,' she said"; "He gave me that look again"; "She looked as if she might cry"; "She was quite good-looking"—the repetition is still boring. Here are some *possible* changes: " 'See here,' she said"; "He glanced at me that way again"; "I thought she might cry"; "She was quite attractive." But I won't arbitrarily delete or change this word or that; maybe they'll all go, maybe they'll all stay. Each one becomes a separate case to consider in the ongoing search for the right word. Like many writers, I'm not inclined to recognize my own failings, even when they're habitual or seem obvious. Maybe I'm too involved in the forward motion of the story, or I simply can't see the trees for the forest. But of course I can always easily spot mistakes in someone *else's* work. And I'm (grudgingly) grateful when someone spots them in mine.

In the final stage of revision, grammar and syntax should be addressed. There are several excellent guidebooks on usage and style, and there just might be a talented grammarian in your workshop, as there was in one of mine. Trained as an English teacher, Ruth could set you straight on some of the most common errors writers make, such as confusing "lie" and "lay," "her" and "she," and—my own bête noire—"I" and "me." Jean Stafford had such an aversion to the misuse of the word *hopefully* (as in "Hopefully, the enemy will not invade our camp") that she had a sign posted outside her front door: "All hopefully abandon, ye who enter here." Writers should be able to identify a split infinitive or a dangling participle and have a thorough understanding of correct English usage. Having said that, I must add that I don't adhere to meticulous grammar if it interferes with the style or character of a work of fiction. It's possible to be *too* correct, to homogenize work until the writer's voice is lost. There are times when it's absolutely fine to end a sentence with a preposition or split an infinitive. As Raymond Chandler once wrote defiantly to his editor, "When I split an infinite, God damn it, I split it so it will stay split."

I've heard a rumor that the word *whom* is gradually being removed from the language. But doesn't the salutation "To Who It May Concern" look funny on the page? I'll keep using "whom" in that context until "who" seems to be the natural choice. And against the advice of some experts, I'm also in the habit (as you may have noticed) of beginning sentences with "And" or "But." I do it if it *sounds* right and best suits my meaning and the rhythm of the sentences. Freedom from the constraints of perfection is especially important when writing dialogue or interior mono- logue. Characters (like the rest of us) are apt to make "errors" in their speech, some of them indigenous to their region or their culture. They should be allowed to sound like themselves, not some academic ideal. Workshop members, in my experience, of- ten pick up on dialogue that doesn't sound real or consistent with a character's style.

For some writers, insecurity or fear of closure keeps them fussing over a manuscript that's probably already as good as it's going to be. S. J. Perelman's alleged thirty-seven drafts may be an exaggeration, but the sample manuscript page accompanying his *Paris Review* interview indicates some serious revision. Grace Paley says, about the number of her revisions, "I don't like to count. . . . I do it till it's done." There have been times I wrote so many versions of a manuscript, I actually *lost* count. I've been tempted to scribble just a few more changes into my books even when they're bound and in stores—only the threat of arrest for vandalism has stayed my hand. Can you rewrite too much? Certainly. I've seen manuscripts that were so overworked they required a little roughing up rather than more polishing, less gloss and more gristle. It's important to know when to stop revising, when simply to let go. This is an acquired understand- ing, one that may be harder to come by for writers in a work- shop. As long as you keep submitting the work to the group, someone is likely to make suggestions for further revision, if only to keep carrying out his (wearying) role as critic. He may look for symbols that don't exist and become much too analytical. Sometimes, as Freud said, "a cigar is just a cigar."

Editors, too, may be guilty of excessive meddling. My very first published story, the one that got me that Rambler wagon, was considerably altered by the fiction editor at the *Saturday Evening Post*, and not always for the better. I was sent a galley, for my approval, a short time before publication. The first thing I noticed was that the editor had gotten rid of my original title, "The Supermarket Story," and pulled up the first line of the story, "Today a woman went mad at the supermarket," making that the title. This was an excellent change on two counts. Obviously, the new title was more arresting, but my second line (which now became the first line of the story)—"Even now, saying it aloud, or, later, repeating that sentence to my husband, I will see that it is meant to amuse, to attract interest, to get attention"—was a much more unusual and, I believe, intriguing opening. There were some less important, but disagreeable, changes to the middle of the story. For example, in my version, because of her guesswork about another character, the heroine refers to herself as "Hercule Poirot." This was changed to "master detective," for the sake of the reader who might not have heard of Hercule Poirot. "Let him look it up," I grumbled, but only to myself. I was saving my argument for what I considered the worst editorial change to the story—a clause added to the last line. My version ended with "I turned and went into his arms." The editor had tacked on, after a comma, "the only world safe for me and my child at that moment." I objected for two reasons. The first was political; my (emerging) feminist self believed it was possible for women and children to be safe *outside* of a man's embrace. My second reason was purely literary; the add-on was schmaltzy, tell-not-show, and just plain bad writing.

The editor held fast and finally said, firmly, "When you're anthologized, you can do it your way." In other words, as I heard
it, did I still want that Rambler?

I must admit, Dear Reader, that I caved. I crossed out the
addition in my copy of the magazine, but that gave me only minor satisfaction. I've always regretted not following my own in-
stincts and calling the editor's bluff. To make things worse,
every other story I ever published was anthologized *except* for
that one, until, twenty-five years after it first appeared, it was
included in a collection of Bread Loaf writers. This time, belatedly, I did it my way.

Sometimes a writer will cave in to workshop criticism, too.
He may even give all of the comments he receives from the
group equal weight and revise with the hope of pleasing everyone. Audrey Ferber, a writer in California and the member of
two long-standing workshops, says, "In a week when the work is
not going well, or when there have been rejections in the mail, it
is tempting to write for this kind of approval." It's necessary to
remember that this is *your* manuscript, not a collaboration. After seriously considering all of the criticism, only you will decide
what changes, if any, are to be made; your workshop doesn't do
the actual work of revision for you. The self-confidence you gain
over time will allow you to know instinctively when a story is finished and it's time to move on, no matter what anyone says. If
you're still uncertain, you can always set it aside for a while and
work on something else. You're likely to have a fresh perspective when you revisit the troubling story later, and your group
will, too.

5

Writing It Down

I always say, keep a diary and some day it'll keep you.

—MAE WEST

For some reason, I've never been able to keep a formal journal or notebook, although many of my writer friends say it's an invaluable habit. A professional workshop leader I know instructs her group (of beginners) to keep daily notes on their observations and thoughts, what she calls "the minutes of life." She says that the practice enforces the discipline of writing something every day and makes her workshop's members more aware of both themselves and the exterior world. She also encourages them to try writing fiction in journal form, because it's the most intimate form of the first-person narrative, with a chronology that is straightforward and easy to follow.

I've found that certain writers' notebooks (my favorites include Virginia Woolf's, Katherine Mansfield's, and John Cheever's) can be as pleasurable to read as their fiction, as well as illuminating and inspiring about the writing process. You can usually recognize the writer's fictional voice in his personal voice and often see, in a single sentence, or even the merest fragment of a sentence, the initial impulse for a story. Kafka's story "The Metamorphosis" begins:

> *As Gregor Samsa awoke one morning from uneasy dreams*
> *he found himself transformed in his bed into a gigantic*
> *insect.*

"The Metamorphosis" was written in 1913. In 1911, Kafka wrote in his diary:

> *February 19.*
> *When I wanted to get out of bed this morning, I simply*
> *folded up.*

There, then, is the genesis of the story, rooted in experience, but not yet worked by the imagination, or probably even recognized for what it would become two years later.

And in his 1965 book *Journal of the Fictive Life*, an unusual, eclectic record of a poet's creative experience, Howard Nemerov wrote:

> *Book reviewers have got from much reading a clear*
> *impression of what life is like; this clear impression they*
> *professionally apply to showing that the books they read*
> *are not lifelike. That could be a lot better phrased. But so.*

I believe he actually *did* phrase it better in 1973, in this brief poem:

To My Least Favorite Reviewer

When I was young, just starting at our game,
I ambitioned to be christlike, and forgive thee.
For a mortal Jew that proved too proud an aim;
Now it's my humbler hope just to outlive thee.

In Katherine Mansfield's *Journal*, she describes the ecstasy of writing and the frustration of not writing. One entry in which she serves as a cheerleader to her muse—"I make a vow to finish a book this month. I'll write all day and at night, too, and get it finished. I *swear*"—is followed a few days later by this notation: "*Evening.* Have written a good deal." The value of putting things down, even without an obvious, immediate context for them, is evident, so it's not that I don't *want* to follow such models of good working habits. And my dereliction is not out of disdain for the particulars of everyday life, either; I completely agree with the Henry Green character who says that "everything has supreme importance, if it happens." Maybe letter writing has taken the place of the journal for me—I do correspond fairly often with a few writer friends—although I don't keep copies of my own letters for future reference. Or perhaps my inability to keep a regular personal record has something to do with temperament and self-discipline; I've always been pretty lazy and easily distracted. My parents gave me a five-year diary when I was thirteen, and I was enthralled by its inviting blankness— why, my whole life lay before me, just as clean and unused! And I loved the little golden key with which I could lock up my private thoughts, away from my sisters' prying eyes. But I never made it past that first month or so of entries. Maybe what I'd written was boring, even to me; I vaguely remember giving equal space to a mad crush I had on a boy named Artie P. and (after what was apparently a lackluster day) what I'd eaten for dinner. Looking back now, I wish I had persevered. I'm sure it would have made it easier to conjure up an adolescent girl when I was trying to write a novel about one. All of my work probably would have been enhanced by some specific, day-to-day impressions of the world around me. I do recognize the fictional potential of many experiences even as they're happening, but my haphazard way of jotting things down anywhere, from the cover of the phone book to the cover of a matchbook, leaves a lot to chance. Occasionally, I'll find some encoded message to my writer self on the back of an old Bloomingdale's bill: "More turbulent weather indoors than out . . ." "Climbing, hand over hand, out of childhood . . ." "She was beautiful by default. . . ." If there was ever a context for any of these disparate fragments, I've forgotten it by now. And I'll probably never know what I meant by those enigmatic single words scribbled here and there: "Friday?" "Teeth." "Chickens." Even my handwriting is unreliable, making many of those memos indecipherable. They remind me of the note Woody Allen's would-be bank robber hands to a teller in *Take the Money and Run*. Less terrified than puzzled, she struggles to read it. " 'I have a . . . *gub?'* " she finally says.

Some people's journals are simply repositories for gripes and groans, the kinds of kvetching that would drive away their friends and families (not to mention any possible readers). Amy Hempel says, "Looking for catharsis or a way to salve pain is a bad reason to go into fiction [or a workshop!], but it's a good reason to keep a journal." That's why Consuelo Baehr writes in hers first thing every morning. "The stuff I write in my notebook," she says, "is effortless true 'stream of consciousness' writing that's indulgent but serves a purpose." That expressed purpose is to "clear the decks" for her "real" writing.

A journal or diary or notebook is usually a personal chronicle of daily events and often a first attempt at the written narrative. It's a routine that's often begun in childhood and continued by some people throughout their lives. Not everyone who keeps a regular record of his days becomes a writer, but it does encourage the habits of observation and interpretation that often lead to that profession. And because you are your journal's only intended reader (in most cases; some people clearly write theirs for posterity), you can play with establishing a fictional voice without self-consciousness or fear of criticism. Its only major pitfall is a necessarily narrow vision of the world, as in any first-person narration, but you can offset that by quoting directly from others you encounter in art and in life, as Joyce Carol Oates does. In her journals she carries on dialogues with writers past and present, as well as with herself. One entry: "*Why write?* To read what I've written. *Why read what you've written?* Because, for all its possible flaws and omissions, no one else could have written it."

Joan Didion has kept a notebook for years. Like me, she's puzzled by many of the jottings she made in the past, so she's given up what she calls "pointless" entries. "Instead," she says, "I tell what some would call lies." (I would call them fictional truths.) And despite all the observations of others she's recorded, she recognizes that the purpose of her notebook is to "remember what it was to be me: that is always the point." Gail Godwin, who made her first diary out of notebook paper, cardboard, and yarn when she was thirteen, and has filled a series of diaries since then, admits to a similar exploration of self. She says that she began the ritual of diary keeping "because I felt there was nobody else like me and I had to know why—or why not." Gloria Naylor, another early diarist, was given her first diary ("the kind with a cheap lock your sister could open with a bobby pin") by her perceptive mother, who recognized that her nontalkative daughter needed an outlet for her thoughts and feelings.

For other writers, the custom is less personal and more pragmatic. Judy Blume always keeps a notebook directly related to the next book she's planning to write, a kind of prewriting ritual. She considers it her "security blanket." Anything that occurs to her about character development or plot gets written into the notebook first. When the notebook is filled, she's ready to start writing the novel. Ella Leffland calls her notebook a "thought book," although it also contains descriptions, essays, scraps of ideas, impressions of books, and "all sorts of meandering." Judith Rossner refers to her "not-a-journal," which contains only a few personal entries. The rest, like Judy Blume's, are work related and include these assorted bits of wit and wisdom:

> *I've come to believe that children raised according to any theory get more messed up than others.*

> *S's losing his Greek when his tonsils were removed.*

> *To be Opened Only After my Death, by Paula Jones.*

> *She'd had a string of husbands and in between them a couple of men she'd loved.*

J.J. re her mother-in-law: "I think she says nice things
about us behind our backs."

Rossner's jottings appear to contain the seeds for at least one contemporary novel. If you're writing period fiction, reading other novels or straight histories written about the same era can give you hints about its flavor and rhythms, as well as a chronicle of some actual events. But I've found that reading journals and notebooks kept during the same period have even more value. The quality of time and place is enhanced by that essential human interpretation. The diarist says what the fiction writer tries to convey, via her characters: *this is what it feels like to be me, here and now.*

Novelist Marnie Mueller says that her faithfully kept journal has served her in different ways. She writes down everything she can recall of her days (and nights), including verbal exchanges, thoughts, feelings, and dreams, the negative along with the positive. In that way, she's able to exorcise temporarily those parts of her life—private worries; family arguments, with their residual anger and distress—that distract her from her work. Keeping a journal, Mueller states, also tones her writing muscles. A written sentence is a written sentence, no matter where or why it's recorded.

Katherine Anne Porter filled numerous volumes of her journal and came to this conclusion (written in one of them) about the practice.

I keep notes and journals only because I write a great
deal, and the habit of writing helps me to arrange,
annotate, stow away conveniently the references I may

need later. Yet when I begin a story, I can never work in
any of those promising paragraphs, those apt phrases,
those small turns of anecdote I had believed would be so
valuable.

This insight was not her *final* entry, however, so journal keeping had to have offered its own mysterious uses and comforts. Maybe it provided the discipline of daily writing. And maybe her notations led her to those paragraphs, phrases, and anecdotes she *did* use in her fiction.

In an odd familial twist, William Wordsworth found his sister Dorothy's journal to be invaluable to his own writing. He mined her notations, copying sentences into *his* notebook and developing poems from them, often using her very words. I can't help thinking she would have benefited from one of those little golden keys like the one that protected the privacy of my girlhood diary. But apparently her brother's literary poaching didn't disturb Dorothy Wordsworth at all; she continued to keep her journal for the express purpose of pleasing him. It's hard to imagine such sibling devotion and generosity.

Frederick Busch has always kept a notebook with him, even at his bedside, and he insists that his students do the same, because "you lose things." One's thoughts, he says, are as ephemeral as dreams, unless you write them down, thereby coaching yourself to be receptive to the subconscious. Of course he's right; you do lose things—ideas, images, language—and it gets worse as you get older. It's like writing with a wet finger on hot pavement (which I once actually tried to do, when a sentence came to me while I was swimming laps in a pool). I used to tell myself that if it was important, I'd remember it, but I realize now, gazing into the abyss of all those missing words, that it was an arrogant and ignorant assumption. Writing it down is still the only insurance against the fickleness of memory.

Ted Solotaroff says, "Keeping a journal with some depth to it is a good way to discover and strengthen one's natural style and the best way to talk to oneself about the real issues of one's experience." A woman in a workshop I attended always kept a journal of its proceedings. She said that reading her entries later reconnected her to a way of thinking critically, which, in turn, helped her to revise her fiction. It might be interesting to inquire about the journal-keeping habits of your workshop's members. Are those who write something personal every day more disciplined in their fiction writing? And does their work seem especially introspective and insightful?

Since I began writing this chapter, I've taken out one of the blank books I've received as gifts over the years and began scribbling in it. So far it looks a lot like those phone books and matchbooks I'm more used to writing on: a collection of somewhat disjointed and mostly illegible thoughts and observations. I'll just have to wait and see what develops. If nothing else, it may be fun to (try to) read what I've written someday. An Oscar Wilde character who takes his diary along whenever he travels says, "One should always have something sensational to read on the train."

6

Troubleshooting

Where there is much desire to learn, there of necessity will be much arguing, much writing, many opinions; for opinion in good men is but knowledge in the making.

—JOHN MILTON

Those of you in leaderless workshops that have survived the initial trials of organization should (and probably do) feel proud of yourselves. After only a few rough episodes, everything's been going smoothly. People have been showing up regularly and on time, and your group has settled into an amicable and productive routine. Any arguing that's been going on has been the healthy kind, based on an honest difference of opinion, rather than on pettiness or personal animosity.

But then, just as you're becoming complacent, there's trouble in River City. Suddenly, attendance is spotty and your meetings have started to disintegrate into banter and gossip. The same person seems to dominate every single discussion. One member accuses another of betraying the confidentiality of the workshop. Someone else has become overly sensitive and can no longer process or accept criticism. Then little cliques begin to form and those cliques develop a gang mentality—the Jets on one side of the room, the Sharks on the other. A couple of the writers are openly, meanly jealous of each other, and one person insists that somebody's been stealing her work. There are tears, shouting, and recriminations, a kind of epidemic of ill will. For some mysterious reason you've begun to resemble a dysfunctional family at Thanksgiving. This is when you may want to call it quits or when you start wishing you had a leader (parent) in place to resolve the problems and restore order. But with a fair amount of effort and determination, order can be restored by the group itself.

A special housecleaning session, one that's separate from the regular workshop meeting, should be called to address all of the issues. That means no manuscripts, no literary criticism, no book talk at all. This will be a command performance, to be held at a time when *everyone* (implicated in the complaints or not) is able to attend. The evening's host may serve as a kind of moderator who reviews the general workshop rules you've agreed upon and calls on people to speak their hearts and minds. Complaints should be aired one at a time. Everyone with something to say on each matter that's raised should have the chance to do so, but without grandstanding or filibustering. The courtoom atmosphere you've so painstakingly developed for the workshop will serve you well during this special session. But this time the writers as individuals will be "on trial" rather than their work. The following are examples of personality types and traits that can lead to serious workshop problems.

Johnny-Come-Lately (Or Never)

Repeatedly arriving late to the workshop or not showing up at all may reasonably be interpreted as a loss of interest in the group or hostility to some of its members. It's especially discourteous and disruptive to wander in right in the middle of someone else's critique. Genuine excuses, like illness or accidents, are, of course, acceptable. But the guilty party who keeps offering the same weak alibis about last-minute "emergencies," heavy traffic, or delayed baby-sitters must be reminded of the pledge of commitment made when the workshop was first formed. Continuing membership in the group should be regarded as an earned privilege, not a God-given right. Everyone can be held up by unforeseen events once in a while, but chronic latecomers and absentees may be justly warned: three strikes and you're out.

The Life of the Party

Most writers I know are fun to be with; as practiced storytellers, they can usually relate anecdotes with panache and almost never forget the punch line of a good joke. They also have an innate need for an audience. In the early days of a workshop, even the most sociable writers are fulfilled by the response to their written work. But after a while, some irrepressible type may need a faster fix: the laughter that's elicited by a little spontaneous wordplay or witticism, or the thrall that follows a well-executed piece of gossip. The temptation is to mix straight criticism with personal asides and entertaining little vignettes that aren't really relevant to the affairs of the group. I know that I've been guilty of this myself. And it can be contagious. Every anecdote she hears reminds a writer of another one, and so on. Telling stories is so much easier than writing them! And nobody ever criticizes the ones that are just told. Everyone may be having such a good time that only the person whose work was under discussion a few minutes ago realizes what's happened. He shouldn't be shy about interrupting the revelry to remind everyone of the business at hand: "Hey, forget about your Aunt Tillie and that hilarious incident at the laundromat; let's get back to my story."

The Boss

Some people are naturally aggressive and aggressively garrulous. They have either more to say than others or just a more elaborate and commanding way of saying it. They tend to take over, to hold everyone else captive to the sound of their voices. In social situations, this can be amusing, even mesmerizing, but it is overbearing in the democracy of a writing workshop. If a member confronted with his own loquaciousness apologizes and promises more self-control in the future, you'll just have to wait and see if he's true to his word. Anyone who admits to inappropriate behavior and seems genuinely contrite about it should be given another chance. But if he denies that he's talking too much and then continues doing it, it may be a matter of misperception: fiction writers are prone to different views of the same event. You might want to tape a few sessions (with everyone's consent), to be played back as evidence at a future troubleshooting session. The talker might also plead guilty but claim extenuating circumstances, for example, that the level of criticism has deteriorated and it's his mission to resurrect it, single-handedly. In that case, the cooperative nature of the workshop probably needs to be reiterated, but the countercomplaint should be addressed, too, with a discussion of possible remedies. Has there been too much unnecessary nitpicking? Should more attention be paid to larger creative issues, like structure or character development? How can your meetings be enlivened and enriched? You might ask yourselves if you've fallen into a comfortable, but boring, pattern of behavior. A good way to break the monotony is to hold occasional focus sessions, especially when there's no backload of manuscripts (see chapter 9). In any event, the person who's been shown to dominate the group should be asked to exercise more restraint. If necessary, parliamentary procedure may be put into practice until courtesy and mutual respect are reestablished.

Transference

In one workshop I attended many years ago, a young woman I'll call Gail ran from the room in tears in the middle of the critique of her story. She was so upset she was unable to talk about it that evening, or during any of the sessions that followed. The whole group suffered from a kind of free-floating anxiety after that. Everyone was especially careful in any further discussion of Gail's work, so she never received another completely honest response to it. People buzzed about the incident for weeks, falling into little splinter groups that took sides with either Gail or her critic, and eventually the workshop disbanded. I met Gail again recently and asked if she'd be willing to talk about that experience now. She said she still remembers it with embarrassment and pain, but as the social worker she's since become, she has a belated perspective on what happened. She maintains that the criticism of her story *was* unnecessarily rough but that she probably overreacted—a response triggered by the fact that the man who offered it reminded her of her father, who'd deserted the family when she was a child. It would have been counterproductive if she'd explained all that in the workshop, even if she had understood it then. The story of her life would distract everyone from the story she'd presented for analysis, and, even in those exceptional circumstances, the workshop should not dissolve into group therapy. Instead, she might have simply said that she'd been having some personal problems and that her extreme reaction was displaced. As to her complaint about the severity of the criticism, it probably would have been useful to open that subject for immediate discussion. Maybe she was just blindsided by her emotions. Or maybe her critic forgot that the manuscript, not the writer, is up for commentary and that the words we use to talk about writing should be as thoughtfully chosen as those we use when we write. You don't have to be ultrasensitive to take offense if, for instance, someone calls your work "slutty" or "stupid" (words I've actually heard used in workshop situations).

Trust Breaking

When I interviewed fellow writers for this book, I especially sought anecdotes about their workshop experiences that I hoped would be helpful to other groups. To my conflicted feelings of disappointment and admiration, some writers who are still members of ongoing workshops said they had interesting stories to tell but were unable to tell them without breaking the trust of the group. Those who did relate anecdotes were careful not to name names or give any other identifying information. Unfortunately, not everyone is so conscientious or trustworthy. Any participant who can't resist telling tales outside of the workshop seriously violates the original commitment made to the other members. (She's like the juror who gossips about a case before it's settled.) It can be difficult, once the trust is broken, to feel comfortable and safe with one another again. It's up to the group to decide whether the transgressor should get another chance or simply be asked to leave.

The "In" Crowd

A woman who used to be a workshop enthusiast told me that she resigned from her group after two other women kept scribbling little notes to each other during the critique of one of her stories. It was just the last in a series of insults; the two women and one of the men passed notes and whispered a great deal every week, and they often fled together as soon as the meeting broke. She came to think of them as the "three witches," always stirring up trouble. "Maybe I was just being paranoid," she said. "Maybe their notes were about somebody or something else, but I still felt hurt. It was like high school all over again, that old business of being 'in' or 'out.' I didn't need that; I didn't want to be popular, just treated fairly. And I didn't trust what any of them said about my work, even when it was positive, because they all always seemed to agree with their buddies." Making friends in a workshop is natural, but forming exclusive little coteries is not. I don't blame this woman for feeling angry and left out, but I think she should have spoken up for herself, and perhaps for others who felt the same way she did. Passing secret notes and exchanging knowing glances and whispers with a few people in a workshop *is* rude and hurtful. Anything one has to say about the manuscript should be addressed *directly* to the writer, and exchanging notes about other matters is only indicative of straying attention. A workshop is not supposed to be high school revisited, and anyone who behaves in such a grossly adolescent way should be called on it and told to stop.

Sibling Rivalry

Most of us, as kids, had occasion to vie with our brothers and sisters for parental attention and approval. I still have a few scars to prove it. A little "sibling" rivalry may take place in writing workshops even without that parent-cum-leader in place and even in the basically noncompetitive atmosphere you've so carefully fostered. Perhaps someone has enjoyed exceptional acclaim from the group, or has had a story accepted for publication. It's not unusual or even unhealthy for someone else to feel a disturbing little pang of envy. It's what one *does* with the feeling that matters. As kids, we threw tantrums, tattled on one another, and even told a few self-promoting lies. As adolescents we resorted to name-calling and blurted out sentiments like "You're just lucky!" and "I hate you!" Grown-ups are supposed to be more civilized and composed, yet I've seen workshop members set themselves up as so-called devil's advocates, offering unreasonably sharp criticism simply to stem or counteract a deluge of praise for another writer. On the other hand, some writers merely *interpret* genuinely thoughtful criticism as jealousy and an attempt to undermine their work. In either case, it can get ugly and improperly personal, just as it did in your childhood family, and you shouldn't be afraid to point that out. An open and frank discussion may reveal questionable motives or baseless defensiveness. Other, uninvolved members might recount how they handled similar situations or offer suggestions for living more comfortably with those disagreeable but not unnatural emotions. In my experience, vying with *famous* writers instead of each other helps to deflect some of that in-house competition, and believe me, Stephen King and Alice Walker aren't likely to get too upset about it.

Yours, Mine, or Ours?

Sometimes it's difficult to identify the original source of a particular quote that keeps appearing in print, with varying permutations and attributions. Each writer who uses this sort of received wisdom puts his own spin and his own stamp on it, until everyone comes to believe *he* made it up. This hardly seems like a crime. T. S. Eliot once said something like "Good writers borrow, but great writers steal." At least I *think* he said it first. In any case, it's hardly comforting to the writer who believes his work has been appropriated by another member of the workshop or to the one accused of appropriating it. It's important to remember that just as we first learn to speak by mimicking our parents, we first learn to write under the influence and through the inspiration of other writers. Often, what seems like blatant piracy is merely an unconscious imitation of work we admire. Children write freely in the "style" of favorite writers and sometimes end up swiping content, too, blithely passing it off as their own. The young Helen Keller unwittingly did it, to her subsequent surprise and chagrin. And Hemingway's first recorded short story, written for his sixth-grade English class, was only a slight variation on an autobiographical tale told to him by his great-uncle. *Hitty*, the book about a doll that I read as a child, was subtitled *Her First Hundred Years*; was it mere coincidence that my own earliest attempt at writing a novel, when I was nine or ten, covered the first hundred years in my human heroine's life?

I remember that right after a best-selling John Irving novel appeared, several of my writing students' stories began to include roller-skating bears, rape, and accidental castration. It wasn't hard to explain, without being too damning, why this "sincerest form of flattery" should be avoided in favor of one's own, original vision—in effect, the world according to *you*. I'm not referring to those deliberate acts of plagiarism mature adults commit, when whole passages are lifted verbatim or are only superficially altered before the heist. That's a very serious trespass, especially in a workshop, where trust is cardinal, and the offender should probably be asked to leave the group, the way students are expelled from universities for the same offense. But some grayer areas of possible misconduct must also be addressed. Someone's novel under discussion takes place in a hospital and, lo and behold, a couple of weeks later someone *else's* incipient novel takes place in a hospital, too. Or, your protagonist turns out to be a translator from the Portuguese, just like mine—what an amazing coincidence! There actually *are* pure coincidences; every publishing season, it seems, two novels with similar themes or characters, or even the same *title*, appear. It's as if a particular premise has simply entered the communal consciousness. The writers may not even be aware of one another's existence until their "related" books are published. Everyone concerned might take heart from Theodore Roethke's observation: "There are only a few bony concepts, but think of the metaphors!" In other words, it's up to each writer— as Ezra Pound suggested—to "make it new." Still, there's uneasiness in a workshop when one writer seems to be adopting another's ideas (or more). All you can really do is talk it over and thereby raise the level of awareness about the issue in your group.

In most instances it pays to air grievances openly, with everyone present and involved in the discussion. Confiding in only one or two members about problems that concern the whole group just contributes to widening whatever fissures already exist in the workshop. But there can be unpleasant consequences to talking things over. Somebody may decide to quit if problems aren't resolved to his satisfaction, or the group may have to ask someone whose actions regularly disturb the cooperative climate to leave. Like certain bad marriages that simply can't be saved, some writing groups are inherently incompatible and will have to disband for its individual members to do well. Even this worst scenario is better than a chronic underground rumbling that threatens to surface and explode and spoils the productivity and spontaneity of the group. And you'll have learned something important for when you form or join your *next* writing workshop.

7

Stuck

God lets you write, he also lets you not write.

— Attributed to Kurt Vonnegut

There's an old saying: "If you neglect your muse for one day, she will neglect you for three," which can only set off alarms in the blocked writer. Judy Blume takes a calmer, more philosophical view. "There are good days and worse days," she says. But for some of us those worse days expand into weeks or months or years. Even the most dedicated of writers can experience a prolonged failure of inspiration or the inability to continue working on something already in progress. In a letter to his brother in 1906, James Joyce wrote, "No pen, no ink, no table, no room, no time, no quiet, no inclination."

On occasion the nonwriting writer can attribute his paralysis to real-life traumas or distractions. Eudora Welty produced only three short stories during the fifteen-year period she cared for her invalid mother. Theodore Dreiser suffered a ten-year artistic paralysis after his publishers withheld on moral grounds the release of his novel *Sister Carrie*. Tillie Olsen, who raised a family without household help, and held a job outside the home as well, didn't publish a book until she was fifty. She writes, "The years when I should have been writing, my hands and being were at other (inescapable) tasks." Illness, poverty, and overwhelming emotional burdens have all contributed to obstructing other writers' careers. Although your workshop isn't the forum for complaining about your personal life, your fellow members may help you to face the writing problem and ultimately resolve it. You're apt to discover that others have been in (and managed to get out of) a similar fix. Just talking about a block to understanding colleagues beats suffering in silence and isolation.

Sometimes there's no apparent reason and no reasonable excuse for a sudden work stoppage. I've heard writers ascribe their stasis to an inability to find the right way to say something, while Tim O'Brien suggests that the so-called blocked writer simply has nothing to say. One thing is certain: when the blank page reflects the blankness of the writer's mind, the effect is chilling. And the torpor seems to feed itself. It's something like the breathlessness experienced while one concentrates too hard on breathing or the insomnia that invariably follows a *fear* of insomnia.

Everyone offers the blocked writer advice, the way people do when you have a cold. But what works best then? Vitamin C? Chicken soup? Zinc lozenges? Staying in bed? Keeping active? Someone will swear by each of these "cures," just as others will advise you to break your writing block in various, often opposing ways. Your group will probably be full of suggestions. Sit down every day and write something, they'll say, or, get up and forget about it for a while. Read. Don't read. Go to the movies. Do little writing exercises. Actually, all of these ideas are sound, in some instances, for *some* writers, while others among us must find our own way out of the crisis. But in the meantime, terror could set in. If the dictionary definition of a writer is "one who writes," doesn't it follow that you're no longer a writer if you're not writing? Not exactly. A considerable part of the process is the dreaming phase, when ideas and language and characters are simmering in the unconscious, not ready yet to rise up and coalesce into actual written prose. Some things can't be rushed; a certain amount of patience is required, as is the belief that *waiting* to write is in itself productive.

In his short story "Love in the Morning," Andre Dubus's hero is a writer who thinks: ". . . and suddenly the sentence was inside me; it had come from whatever place they come from. It is not a place I can enter at will; I simply receive its gifts." I'm of a similar bent. When people ask where my stories come from, I'm inclined to say that if I knew, I'd go there immediately and get a fresh batch. In the meantime, I mostly wait, and wait. . . . My family has threatened to confront me with what they consider my mule-headed procrastination by holding one of those intervention sessions organized by friends and relatives of substance abusers. If only there were such a thing as the Betty Ford Clinic for Blocked Writers!

Many writers consider their workshop a worthy equivalent, a place where recovery (productivity) is stimulated and encouraged. But even habitual workshop attendees can experience a stubborn creative pause. Its origins may be mysterious, and its duration unpredictable (the most frightening aspect), but it happens, and it's not that uncommon. In a particularly poignant entry in what Katherine Mansfield referred to as her "huge complaining diaries," she wrote: "Oh God, my God, let me work! Wasted! Wasted!" Willa Cather had a notable five-year slowdown in her thirties, after a long fertile period, and Thomas Hardy fell into a prose silence for thirty years. "Less and less shrink the visions then vast in me," he lamented. His fictional silence proved terminal, although he did write a great deal of poetry during those last years. Some writers I know switch to penning screenplays, essays, and book reviews to keep their hand in and their spirits up. Tillie Olsen attacked her problem head-on by writing about it in a book aptly called *Silences*, and I'm writing this book during an extended pause in my own fiction writing. Still others engage in writing-*related* activities, like teaching writing (those who can, do; those who can't, teach) and editing.

Many people agree that you can use up your creative energy that way, that you should really look for work in some completely separate field. Mona Simpson recommends that her writing students do volunteer work "to remind them of the larger world they come from, which includes babies, widows, children, old people and orphans, who all have cares and tragedies, accidents and joy." Amy Hempel—who prefers the term "writer's search" to writer's block, because it seems more active—heartily agrees. She volunteered to train guide dogs for the blind to distract herself from her anxiety about not writing. And she chose dog training because it was a worthy cause and hands-on work that had nothing at all to do with writing. But maybe everything we engage in has something to do with writing, because the story that finally broke Amy Hempel's writing "search" turned out to be about guide dogs.

Another strategy is total denial. There used to be an advertising slogan for a brand of packaged bread: "We bake while you sleep." Sometimes, when I'm in the grip of a protracted silence, I tell myself that I'm not really blocked, that I'm writing all the time (just not writing it down), while I'm sleeping and eating and generally involved in what Conrad called the "common joys" of common life. Maybe there's some truth to this desperate theory, since I often find myself in a kind of fugue state when I'm not actively writing, suffering from what my husband calls my "selective deafness," and what I think of as "going inward." And after what seems like an endless dry period, prose sometimes rushes at me in sudden, surprisingly whole and polished passages. Virginia Woolf wrote, "My mind works in idleness. To do nothing is often my most profitable way."

But what do you tell people during that time of "profitable" idleness? The inevitable cocktail party inquiry in any artistic or academic crowd is "What are you working on now?" People who are blocked and don't enjoy casually discussing the problem learn to be evasive. They mention "something in early progress," and say they don't want to talk about it during its fragile "larval" stage. Or they just smile mysteriously and don't say anything at all. As every writer knows, undeveloped story ideas can be spent in conversations about them. Norman Mailer says, "Talking about present work discharges the tension." In any event, it's not that hard to ward off probing questions in a social setting about such a private matter. But for the workshop member, not writing is not a private matter. Although it's natural for some people to be more prolific than others, if you haven't presented a manuscript for several weeks or months, it's bound to be noticed, and you (and others) may begin to question your function and place in the group. Continuing participation in the workshop is *imperative* during a slowdown, if only to keep in touch with the creative action. And the writer who's temporarily lost his writing voice—laryngitis of the soul is the way I think of it—hasn't necessarily lost his critical powers, too. He is still a player, and talking constructively about the work of others can revitalize his own creative juices as well. Members of the group may actually offer *useful* advice or at the very least the solace of their empathy.

It's been said that Hemingway often left off writing for the day in the middle of a sentence so that he'd have a guaranteed place to start the following day. Other writers trick themselves into continuing by not allowing themselves certain pleasures, like dessert or coffee, until they've produced a specified number of pages. One of them says, gloomily, "It's so tempting to try to fill the void with food, and then I'm not only still blocked, I'm fat, too." John Steinbeck advised: "Abandon the idea that you are ever going to finish. . . . Write just one page for each day, it helps. Then when it gets finished, you are always surprised."

Susan Isaacs fights off spells of creative inertia by forcing herself to sit at her desk for at least two hours every morning, trying to write something, *anything.* It sounds like a valid method because, as most of us know, even faulty starts can eventually lead to good writing. Essayist Jo Ann Beard says she sometimes has trouble sleeping at night, especially when she's excited by ideas for her work, but whenever she's blocked, she drops off within minutes of attempting to write. I, too, have found myself crashed out on the keys of my computer on a fallow day. When I told Susan Isaacs that her two-hour scheme wouldn't work for me because of my habit of falling asleep at the switch, she sternly advised me to deduct my sleeping time and restart the clock. I still prefer standing around and waiting for inspiration, even though I'm more likely to be hit by a falling safe than by an idea. What else do I do when I'm not writing? I anguish about it a lot, and of course I read. I try not to be envious of friends whose typing fingers peck mercilessly against my very heart, and I take courage from Faulkner's assurance that "if a story is in you, it has got to come out."

But after a while, I fall prey to other distractions, like talking on the telephone, or browsing in thrift shops. Kelly Simon, a writer in San Francisco with similar shopping habits, says, "I go from thrift shop to thrift shop and relentlessly buy clothes I don't need until I'm so disgusted with myself that I'm driven back to the computer out of guilt." But maybe we're not just shopping; maybe we're in search of someone else's nostalgia, a story hidden in the folds and seams of their discarded clothing. Or maybe I'm just trying to put a good spin on what is merely a shameful delaying tactic.

Anne Roiphe likens the creative impulse to a car battery that runs down if you don't keep driving. I know that I've been rewarded after determinedly sticking with an iffy project by a sudden turn for the better, an unexpected infusion of inspiration and energy. Having more than one main character in a novel has proved to be useful when I'm experiencing a slowdown; it's easier to pick up a stalled story from another viewpoint. Switching back and forth between points of view can even allow you to present the same scene in different versions, in the tradition of *Rashomon.* Another trick that's worked for me is leaping ahead in the chronology and writing a scene (preferably one in which the heroine is born, dies, or falls madly in love) that engages me more than the one on which I've been stuck. This is probably the grown-up version of the way I read as a child, seeking out the "good" parts in a book first.

In extreme cases of writer's block, psychotherapy is a feasible approach. The writer may need help to recognize and overcome his fear of failure or his inability to "banish the critic" (as we used to say in workshop) *before* he starts to write. Another possible bugaboo is the fear of success, which afflicts people in every field. Those who want to be liked more than admired or envied, especially in a workshop, may unconsciously thwart their own chance of succeeding by not writing at all. Success also presents the real challenge of maintenance, which is probably why so many writers get jammed when it comes to their second novels. And then there's the fear of facing the *content* of one's fiction, which might evoke painful thoughts or memories. William Gass puts it best in his essay, "The Doomed and the Sinking": "Writing. Not writing. Twin terrors. Putting one's mother into words. . . . It may have been easier to put her in her grave."

Couples seeking sex therapy are often told to indulge in foreplay, but abstain from intercourse. Similar advice is given to writers who've lost their creative libido: Doodle, write in your notebook, do little character sketches, but by all means don't go back to your novel until your confidence and creative flow are restored. Writers stumped for ideas or for the technique of telling a particular story may want to recall the circumstances preceding some of their former productive spells. Like, "What were you doing, Mr. Melville, when that whale first swam into your consciousness?" Reading is a stimulus for some of us, who just need to be refueled with written language. History books can inspire historical fiction. Reading mysteries may arouse the literary detective in you. And newspaper items can spark fictional concepts, as they did for Dinitia Smith (*The Illusionist*), Rosellen Brown (*Before and After*), Sue Miller (*While I Was Gone*), and Robert Olen Butler (*A Good Scent from a Strange Mountain*). Novelist and playwright Elizabeth Dewberry saves newspaper clippings to browse through when she's short of ideas for new work. She says that local newspapers are the best source because they give more space to smaller, quirkier human-interest stories. An article in a Lake Charles, Louisiana, paper, about "lawn crypts," an innovative burial practice in which bodies are stacked aboveground, gave rise to a Dewberry play about a couple of newlyweds given just such a "bunk-bed" funeral plot by the groom's mother as a wedding present. You can imagine the comic possibilities: mother-in-law jokes (she chooses our China pattern, and now *this*), who will be on top for eternity, et cetera. In *The Making of the Poet*, Paul Zweig says that Walt Whitman, the journalist, was influenced by the "instantaneousness" of the newspaper, which removed everything but the present moment. If external stimuli don't get you going, perhaps rereading your own earlier stories will help you reconnect with your writing voice.

After her third book, Amy Tan couldn't seem to get her new one under way. But she wasn't blocked in the usual sense. In fact, she had *too* much material—enough for the beginnings of five different novels—but the inability to focus properly kept her from concentrating on a single project. She addressed the problem, which she dubbed "environmentally induced attention deficit disorder," more aggressively after an inspiriting conversation about it with Oscar Hijuelos. He even inscribed a copy of his novel *Empress of the Splendid Season* to her with the following:

> *For Amy Tan,*
> *Don't forget the zen way to Tibetan perfection of writing*
> *aesthetics and higher calling:*
>
> *1)   No newspaper before 2 PM.*
> *2)   No e-mail, telephone, no human conversation,*
> *   doggies OK.*
> *3)   No sex, except with husband but even so no emoting.*
> *4)   If stuck, read and then try again.*
> *5)   Drink carbonated water and listen to the radio at low*
> *   volume.*
> *6)   Mantra: Focus, focus, focus, and: I will allow no*
> *   distraction.*
> *7)   Write until 2 PM starting at 10 AM.*
> *8)   Goal: 500 words daily.*
>
> *Once you have honored these rules, which I got from the*
> *High Lama himself in Tibet, you will finish book and settle*
> *into a state of irrepressible bliss.*
>
> *With love and admiration,*
> *Oscar Hijuelos*

Amy Tan says, "Believe me, it worked!" She also applies other disciplines to her daily routine. She attends to her physical self by doing yoga regularly, and she listens to relaxation tapes, which "guide" her to sleep from which she wakes refreshed and ready to plunge into work. Other tapes help to blot out the external world while she's writing. Her most inventive and effective approach is to keep an imaginary hollowed-out book, like the ones in which people hide their valuables. Amy Tan's bottomless "book-safe," is the repository for any personal thoughts or problems that are interfering with her writing. She says that everything usable in her life goes into the book she's writing; the rest goes into the hollow book, and she's able to close its cover firmly on those distracting elements.

Another writer I know, who lives in a noisy metropolitan area, uses a white noise machine to help him focus, as he says, "on the noises in my head." Several writers spoke of doing physical exercises—like running, aerobics, or using a treadmill or an Exercycle—before sitting down to write, claiming that these are both head-clearing and oxygenating practices. Other writers, like Oscar Hijuelos and Amy Tan, go to their desks immediately in the morning, without even the customary delaying tactics of reading the newspaper or turning on the TV news. As Tan eloquently puts it, "I go directly from dream to dream."

The most dispiriting thing about writing fiction is that, in most instances, no one has asked you to do it. Lucy Ellman says, "Writing a novel without being asked seems a bit like having a baby when you have nowhere to live." There are more than fifty thousand new books published each year; does the world really need yours, too? The freelance writer doesn't have the spur of carrying out a superior's command, the way a soldier or an accountant does. I find that the old good-girl syndrome kicks in when I'm writing against a deadline, inspiring both the impulse to please by being on time and the fear of not giving satisfaction. Therefore, I'm never late with a book review or an essay promised for a specific date.

I taught at the Bread Loaf Writers' Conference for a number

of years, and each summer—like everyone else on the faculty—I was required to give a reading, approximately one hour long, of *new* fiction. In addition, I had to prepare a fresh lecture of equal length on some aspect of the craft. For a chronically blocked writer, these preparations were both torture and a healthy spur to start writing again. I loved going to Bread Loaf each August. It was such a joy to be reunited with friends from previous years in the beautiful Green Mountains of Vermont, and I felt a solemn obligation to meet all the requisites of the job.

The invitation to return the following summer usually came shortly after the end of the conference. The year stretched luxuriously before me—I had *plenty* of time to write something new. But then, the months sped by the way they do in those movies that depict time's passage with the flying leaves of a calendar. If I hadn't started writing by March or April, I'd start to worry. I'd sit gloomily at my desk and think of Snoopy, poised on the roof of his doghouse, typing, yet again, "It was a dark and stormy night. . . ." By June, I would be really antsy, and by July I'd be in a full-blown panic. Maybe I'll break my leg or something, I'd think desperately, so I won't *have* to go to Vermont. But the thought of not going broke my heart. Then the annual miracle occurred. Somehow, I'd get something written just in time. The real miracle, though, was that, on a couple of occasions, what was begun as a frantic effort to keep my job became the beginning of a novel I eventually finished, and even enjoyed writing. Not always, of course. Just as not every visit to an artist's colony is equally productive. I remember getting into bed at one retreat as soon as I arrived (in the early afternoon), as if I were a patient at a sanitorium, and my nurse (muse) was going to arrive any moment with a miracle drug. I even dubbed the place

Magic Mountain. But I *was* there to get better from (or at) something, wasn't I?

I've since discovered that my analogy isn't any more original than my soubriquet for Yaddo. The following poem by fellow Bread Loafer Linda Pastan expresses the sense of invalidism many obstructed writers feel.

Block

*I place one word slowly
in front of the other,
like learning to walk again
after an illness.
But the blank page
with its hospital corners
tempts me.
I want to lie down
in its whiteness
and let myself drift
all the way back
to silence.*

It strikes me while writing this that deadlines can be self-imposed, even when no one else is waiting for the manuscript. You might send yourself an imaginary letter of blackmail: "Write something by July 1, or else!" or you might commit yourself to a specific date for presenting a manuscript in your workshop. And if the blocked writer keeps a notebook related to his work, he could read aloud from his daily scribbles in his workshop, in the hope that someone else will recognize the germ of a story. Or he could deviate from his usual narrative style and try writing a story or novel in the form of a diary or journal, as Gogol did in

"Diary of a Madman," Hugh Nissenson in *The Tree of Life*, and Helen Fielding in *Bridget Jones's Diary*. So in the end I find myself siding (at least intellectually) with those who advise the blocked writer to force herself to write something, under any circumstances. As Christina Rossetti said, "Can anything be sadder than work left unfinished? Yes; work never begun."

8

From Craft to Commerce

*Some said, John, print it; others said, Not
so.
Some said, It might do good; others said,
No.*

—John Bunyan,
"Author's Apology",
for *The Pilgrim's Progress*

No matter how pure of heart we claim to be, and no matter how committed to the pursuit of literary excellence, commerce—in the seductive form of publication—eventually enters the minds of most writers. This often happens much too soon, before we've even begun to perfect our craft. The novelist Joseph Heller readily admitted to such early ambition, flatly stating that he only started writing because he wanted to be published. Fortunately, his talent was equal to his impatience, which makes him an exception to the rule, and I suspect his work was fairly polished before he sent it out. Most beginners should probably be less impulsive. It's not a bad practice to put those seemingly perfect new stories into a drawer for a month or so, then take them out and reconsider them with a fresh perspective. Chances are they'll need some revising before they're thrust into the cold, cruel world of publishing.

One does hear stories of nurturing editors, at certain literary magazines and publishing houses, who correspond for years with promising young writers, reading their work in progress, offering criticism and encouragement, and finally taking something on. My own daughter, the novelist Meg Wolitzer, was precocious enough to write and submit her first full-length effort to a major publisher when she was only sixteen. The wise and generous editor who read it told her that she was clearly gifted, but (unsurprisingly) not adequately developed yet as a writer. He said that she could probably find someone willing to publish her manuscript for the sensation her tender age would create, but that it would be a bad career move for her. He went on to predict that she would write something better and more mature before long, and that she'd be glad she waited to publish. Of course she was crushed—it was, after all, a rejection, albeit a gentle one—but she was emotionally mature enough then to follow his advice, and when her first novel, *Sleepwalking*, appeared six years later, just after she graduated from college, it was taken seriously for its literary merits, not just for the phenomenon of her youth.

For most new writers, submitting work prematurely can be truly detrimental, especially in the current, fiercely competitive market. Without an agent or a strong recommendation from a known writer, your manuscript probably won't even be read. And if it *does* get a reading and is summarily dismissed, it will be much harder to attain a second reading after some belated revision. Editors and agents tend to remember names, and later work by the same writer might not be taken seriously, either.

The other danger lies in the despair that comes with repeated rejection. Of course we all have to learn to endure rejection because it's the usual fate of new writers, even those who ultimately go on to publish. Saul Bellow, James Joyce, Marcel Proust, and Beatrix Potter are among the luminaries who took their lumps in the beginning. Even *Peter Rabbit* was rejected! William Kennedy's Pulitzer Prize–winning novel, *Ironweed*, was turned down by thirteen publishers before it was finally accepted, and when Rudyard Kipling was twenty-four, someone at the *San Francisco Examiner* wrote to say, "I'm sorry, Mr. Kipling, but you just don't know how to use the English language." A former student of mine, whose short story recently took first prize in a literary magazine competition, told me that the same story had been regularly rejected for the previous five years.

I've accrued enough rejection slips myself, over the years, to paper a small bathroom. My workshop buddies and I often compared turndowns and then commiserated with one another. Writing well, we decided, was the best revenge, but it was easy to become disheartened. Form letters were the most frustrating because they didn't respond in any discernible way to the particular manuscripts we'd sent. There were no brownie points for characterization or style and no invitations to submit future work. In fact, there wasn't a solitary personal word. I once licked the signature on a note to see if it had been handwritten or merely stamped. On the other hand, a genuine letter from *Playboy* magazine, in its (and my own) early days, was painfully specific, stating that my story was "well-written, but too female-oriented and suburban-situated" for their pages. A few weeks later I was informed that the same story was "just too dark for sunny *Woman's Day*." Manuscripts were either kept like hostages or were returned so fast they might have been submitted by boomerang. A friend who eventually became a popular published writer got her story back promptly from a small magazine, with a note attached that said, simply and scathingly, "This is exactly what we hate."

Though some of these responses seem hilarious now, they hurt like hell at the time. And you always remember the worst things that were said about your writing. For a workshop member who's the first in her group to try to publish, there can be the added stigma of stepping out of line. So why expose ourselves to such discomfort, even anguish, before we have to? Because, despite everything, our dreams of glory sometimes outweigh all the horror stories. It's still tempting to get the work out there, to seek fame and fortune and—best of all—readers who actually *volunteer* for the job. I have to admit that being published is fun (at least before the onslaught of public opinion).

When I was nine years old, I belonged to something called the Junior Inspector's Club, an after-school play group sponsored by the New York City Department of Sanitation. The club put out a mimeographed "literary magazine," and I had a poem about winter accepted for publication. Probably *every* poem submitted to them was accepted, but I didn't think about that then. My mother and I were invited to the offices of the Sanitation Department, where I was to be awarded the bonus of a Certificate of Merit. I remember walking hand in hand with my mother down a street lined with garbage trucks that seemed as solemn and official as a military escort, as clearly as I remember the thrill of my first professional acceptance, the one that transformed me from housewife to writer, as if, à la Clark Kent, I'd gone into a phone booth, pulled off my apron, and emerged with a big *W* on my chest. And when a copy of my first novel arrived (several of my neighbors were waiting outside with me for the mailman), I was suffused with parental pride. I ripped off the wrappings, counted its fingers and toes, and passed it around to be admired and cooed over. Then I rushed into the house with it, shoved it onto a bookshelf, and it looked as if it belonged there, just like a regular book! So, having offered all the above caveats about prematurity and rejection, I'll now make some practical suggestions for submitting work for publication.

The first rule is, *cleverness doesn't count*. A manuscript illustrated with little symbols and pictures, or typed in some elaborate font (so easily accomplished on the computer), is more likely to irritate than amuse the professional reader. An editor I know once received a historical novel done entirely in Elizabethan script (with all those funny-looking "s's" and "u's"). And in a wonderful prose piece by the poet Elizabeth Bishop, called the "U.S.A. School of Writing," one student decorates her manuscripts with Christmas seals, and another painstakingly writes his "in large handwriting on small pieces of paper." A story written in lipstick on a brown paper bag might be passed around the office for laughs, but no one will take it seriously. If you wish to receive *positive* attention, send an unadorned, double-spaced, cleanly typed manuscript bordered by generous margins (very much like the copy you submit to your workshop). The pages should be numbered and have a header or footer that identifies the work; a stray page on a busy editor's desk may never be reunited with its mates. Don't fold or staple or bind the manuscript or do anything else to it that makes it hard to read.

In the same vein, a cover letter written in verse or one that lists your hobbies and pets is an absolute turnoff. An informative cover letter is a good idea, but it must be *brief and to the point.* The most important information is your publishing history, if any, and please don't include that poem about your grandmother's death in your junior high school literary magazine, or anything printed by a vanity press. Do *not* offer your own praise for the submitted work, for example, "I'm enclosing my funny, literate, page-turning novel." You'd be surprised how many writers do just that, even including "blurbs" from family members and nonwriter friends. *Do* mention it if you've been referred to this editor by a writer he might recognize and respect, for instance, "Joyce Carol Oates suggested I send you the enclosed manuscript." Secondary-related information, like your MFA from the Iowa Writers Workshop, your scholarship to Bread Loaf, or your tutorial at Princeton with Joyce Carol Oates, may also be included. It's not a good idea to solicit referrals from former writing teachers who never singled out your work for praise or offered to provide such referrals themselves. And asking published writers who are unfamiliar with your work to read it with the purpose of supporting it is an imposition, and one that might very well backfire. Someone I know received such a cruelly negative response to that kind of request, she almost lost all confidence in herself. "Connections" can help, but only if they're genuine and backed up by enthusiasm. If you have nothing substantial to recommend you, the honesty of a simple statement, such as "I hope you will consider the work of a new writer," can be quite appealing.

Manuscripts for children's picture books are generally not accompanied by illustrations. They should be typed like poems, with double-line spaces to indicate where the page turns in the book would be. It's okay to designate (in the margin) what an illustration might depict, but it's not a good idea to collaborate with an artist friend before submitting the manuscript. Publishers prefer to make that match themselves, and, strange as it may seem, many picture book writers never even *meet* the artists who illustrate their books.

Always address your manuscript (of any genre) to a particular editor *by name*. There's something magnetic about mail addressed directly to oneself, while an envelope addressed to an anonymous "Fiction Editor" is likely to end up in a slush pile read by a very junior person, and never passed on up. (Think of mail you receive that's addressed to "Occupant.") Do your homework and try to find out beforehand who would probably be most receptive to your manuscript. Look at books similar to your own in style or content and note who published them. See if the acknowledgments or the dedication page mentions a particular editor or agent. Consult *current* literary market reference books, such as the *LMP*, to see who edits what at which house or periodical and who is open to reading unsolicited submissions (those that do not come to them via reputable agents). Don't depend on last year's listings; editorial staffs can play musical chairs. Someone I know had her novel rejected by the same editor at three different publishing houses! His final note to her read, "Sorry, but I *still* don't like this."

The same guidelines can be used when sending work to an agent. By the way, it *does* really help to have official representation. Besides ensuring that your work will be read, good agents are familiar with the tastes and needs of the publishing houses and serve as matchmakers between individual writers and editors. But an agent is often almost as hard to come by as a publisher. The reference books that list publishers and magazines also list ethical authors' agents and spell out their methods of operation. For instance, there may be a range in commissions charged, and some agencies, like some publishers, only handle nonfiction or technical books. There are agents who charge a reading fee, and those who suggest sending a letter of inquiry before you submit a manuscript. That letter, like the cover letter to editors, should be brief and pertinent. You might describe your novel as a "historical romance" or "a literary mystery," rather than offer a lengthy synopsis, and don't submit a sample chapter unless you're invited to do so. Nonfiction submissions usually require much more detail. If you're submitting a collection of short stories (which are generally more difficult to place than novels) and you have a novel on the back burner, you should certainly mention that. (Related or linked short stories, with the same cast of characters, like Melissa Bank's *The Girls' Guide to Hunting and Fishing* and Susan Minot's *Monkeys*, may either pass as novels or have the same allure.)

Self-addressed, stamped envelopes, to either agents or editors, ensure return of your unaccepted manuscripts. While you may not care, in this day of cheap and easy duplication, about getting your pages back, this observation of the rules indicates to the addressee that you're a professional. A word count, which I've seen on many student manuscripts, isn't really necessary; that can easily be estimated. It's also unnecessary and may even appear paranoid to claim copyright or first American serial rights on your title page. Editors are not inclined to steal ideas from writers, but if you still feel insecure, you can always register your manuscript with the Writers Guild of America (either the East or West division) for a nominal fee. You don't have to be a guild member, and even outlines or ideas can be registered. If you're sending things out on your own, keep a careful record of where it's been, including dates and the names of the editors who've sent it back. Later on, if a literary agent agrees to represent your work, and a particular manuscript has already made the rounds of a few publishers, you should reveal that history to the agent. It would be embarrassing for her to submit a manuscript to someone who has already rejected it.

Some editors and agents keep manuscripts (unread, I suspect) for months and months. I once submitted a children's book to a publisher who held on to it for more than two *years*. And then it came back with a note that began, "This may seem like a long time . . ." By then, of course, I'd almost forgotten I'd sent it, and I wasn't particularly heartened by the claim that it had been "under serious consideration" all that time. Although you should be patient—most editors attend to various corporate duties during office hours; they aren't just sitting at their desks reading and editing—it's not unreasonable to inquire about your manuscript's status about eight weeks after submission, preferably by mail rather than by phone. (Manuscripts do get lost, even if it takes six trips to the wastebasket to lose one.) You may also want to consider making multiple submissions, and if you do so, be sure to mention it in your cover letter. Most of the editors and agents I've spoken to on the subject don't object to the practice if the writer is up front about it.

At one time, there were many large-circulation magazines that published literary fiction. Writers, even new ones, could hope to be paid handsomely for a story, get a wide readership, and be invited by publishers to dust off that novel manuscript in the closet and send it in. Now, alas, the *Saturday Evening Post* is gone, *Mademoiselle* has replaced their fiction with extended fashion tips, and *Harper's* magazine only prints short excerpts of longer works. The *Atlantic Monthly* and the *New Yorker* are still publishing good stories, and a few newcomers, like *Double-Take* and Francis Ford Coppola's *Zoetrope*, solicit literary fiction, too. But competition is strenuous for space in these prestigious places, so don't overlook the smaller literary magazines. Sections of novels-in-progress that are hard to place elsewhere have a better chance in that lower-keyed market, as do stories that are unconventionally long or simply unconventional. Payment may just be in copies, and the distribution more modest, but many fine writers have debuted in "little" magazines, where confirmed and brand-new talent are often presented back-to-back. I remember reading a chapter of *Ironweed* in a magazine called *Epoch*, before I'd ever heard of William Kennedy. Later, when I read the novel in its entirety—and some of the attendant praise for it—I had the pleasant illusion of having "discovered" Kennedy, although the editors of *Epoch*, and Saul Bellow and Doris Grumbach, who were both enthusiastic and influential champions of his work, actually earned that distinction.

But don't think that placement of a strong story in a literary magazine is a sure thing. Ladette Randolph, the managing editor and senior fiction reader at *Prairie Schooner*, receives more than three thousand stories a year and accepts only about twenty of them. The odds are clearly against the writer who sends his work out, but people keep buying lottery tickets at even greater odds, and submitting your work shows faith in yourself, not just in dumb luck.

What are the editors looking for? The answer to that question varies. Ladette Randolph writes, "We are voyeurs, endlessly fascinated by glimpses into the mysteries of human consciousness through writing that is passionate and distinctive." David Hamilton, the editor of the *Iowa Review*, says, "The first thing to catch me, usually, is voice." The editors at *Northwest Review* ask only for "Quality in whatever form," while those at the *Low-*

ell Review are much more specific: "We are chiefly interested in work that reflects what it is like to live, labor, bleed, sweat, die, and everything in between." Whew! There does seem to be one consensus of editorial opinion: It's a good idea to read recent copies of any publication before submitting work to it.

I was a workshop member when my first short story was bought, and I was in yet another workshop when my first novel was accepted for publication. It's great to be able to share one's success with friends and colleagues. Most of them are genuinely pleased for you and take encouragement from your having arrived. Others, however, may feel jealous, despite the usually good-spirited, noncompetitive atmosphere of the workshop. This is especially true if good luck shines on one of the younger or less experienced writers in a group. (It's something like the youngest daughter in a family marrying before her older sisters.) In the workshop, resentment of your success is less likely if you've been just as forthcoming about previous rejection. In any case, it's best to be reasonably modest after your announcement and then go on with the business of the group. You also have to stop hugging yourself long enough to start contemplating your next writing project. And you might finally be humbled by the experience of publishing, anyway.

When I finished typing the final draft of my first novel, my family and I went out for Chinese food to celebrate. The strip of paper in my fortune cookie read, "Your talents will soon be recognized and rewarded." I'm not particularly superstitious, but I was delighted by that auspicious prediction, and I taped it to my typewriter as soon as we came home. A few years later, after I finished writing my second novel, we went out for Chinese food again. This time my fortune said, "Life is a struggle." That seemed a lot closer to the truth, so I taped it to my typewriter, too. The writing life *is* a struggle, of one kind or another: to find the right words and the time and place to put them down, to accept criticism and rejection, and then do the whole thing all over again. Automatic writing is the equivalent of a free lunch; there is no such thing. My editor Michael di Capua used to remind me when I griped about facing the umpteenth revision, "The book that writes itself may have to read itself." Maybe we should all type *that* one up and tape it to the doors of our workshops.

Part Two

Focus Sessions

9

Talking It Over

That is the happiest conversation where there is no competition, no vanity, but a calm quiet interchange of sentiments.

—SAMUEL JOHNSON

I f your workshop starts to become a little boring, or if there aren't enough manuscripts to fill an entire evening, it may be time to deviate from the usual routine and hold a few focus sessions. These special meetings will provide the opportunity to discuss some of the common challenges of writing fiction and to exchange ideas and share experiences. If you don't want to devote entire sessions to such general discussions about craft, you may simply set aside time at the end of your regular meetings for this purpose. In either case, you can indulge in the airing of individual problems without having to present a manuscript. Talking about fiction without referring to an actuál text can be quite liberating. Most people tend to be more open and less defensive when the conversation isn't directed critically at anyone's work (especially their own).

I once asked a mystery writer in our group to talk about the particular structure of suspense novels. I wasn't planning to write one at the time, but I thought her methods might help with my own problems of plotting, and they did. Someone else wanted to know how to write something funny and how to know when it isn't. There was a lot of laughter, interspersed with groans, at that meeting, and even though none of us went on to become Perelmans or Dorothy Parkers, we all began to understand the origins and purposes of humor. One time, my group spent an entire session on punctuation, those seemingly arbitrary and innocuous squiggles and dots. I particularly remember an example someone gave of the importance of the lowly comma. "Take the comma out of the sentence 'I'm roasting, father,' and you've created a case of patricide." Someone else quoted F. Scott Fitzgerald, who said, "Cut out all those exclamation marks. An exclamation mark is like laughing at your own joke."

Among the other areas that have come up for scrutiny in focus sessions I've attended are character development, fictional voice, plot, dialogue, landscape, humor, writing for children, the differences between short stories and novels, problems in writing about sex, the value of writing exercises in the workshop, and adapting one's stories for the movies or television. The following chapters offer some thoughts on these topics to help you get started in your own discussions.

To prepare for your group's focus sessions:

- Make a list of those areas you feel are weak in your own work, so you can suggest the subject for a future meeting.
- Bring examples of other people's published work you believe successfully (or unsuccessfully) demonstrate the subject under discussion.
- Find and bring to the workshop examples of *other* kinds of creative expression (photographs, drawings, recordings of music) that achieve what you hope to achieve through writing, for example, depiction of character, landscape, or mood.
- Try not to refer to your own work, except in a general way. ("How does one keep characters from sounding exactly alike?" or "I wish I knew how to get a visual image without so much statistical detail.")

You may be surprised to discover that you're not alone in your uncertainties about a particular aspect of writing fiction and that talking it over in your workshop can be truly edifying. As the British critic Sydney Smith once noted, "What you don't know would make a great book."

10

And Then What Happened?

We inherit plots. . . . There are only two or three in the world, five or six at most. We ride them like treadmills.

—JANETTE TURNER HOSPITAL

When I was a child, my father habitually fell asleep in the middle of telling me a bedtime story, and I never hesitated to poke or kick him awake, demanding to know what happened next. What happens next is every story's lure, the thing that drives readers through the pages, careening recklessly around the corners of the plot. But what about the writer? Should he be just as compelled by the plot of the story he's writing, and how much does he have to know up front? These are good questions to raise in your workshop, especially during a focus session.

Donald Barthelme said, "Writing is a process of dealing with not-knowing, a forcing of what and how." John Updike says that he begins his novels with "some kind of solid, coherent image, some notion of the shape of the book and even its texture." Although he doesn't begin until he knows the beginning and has a sense of what's going to happen, he allows for unexpected turns, keeping "a kind of loose rein on the book." Other writers, like John Irving, recommend knowing as much of the story as possible before beginning to write it. He argues, "How can an author make a reader anticipate—not to mention make a reader guess wrong—if the author himself doesn't *know* where a story is going?" In fact, Irving starts writing the actual prose in his head, too, memorizing it as he goes along, until his memory bank is full, and he must rush to write it down. He's referred to this process, amusingly, as the "enema syndrome."

John Gardner used to hang sheets of butcher paper around his writing studio and then outline the plot of his latest novel-to-be on it. The scenario, especially the ending, was subject to change as he began writing and discovered things about his characters and their lives that he didn't know before he began. Well-realized characters often refuse to carry out a preordained plot. But the fundamental progress of events was set in place before Gardner wrote a single word. Conversely (and perhaps perversely) I've always chosen to enter a new novel blindly, with only a vague notion of where it's going. I want to be surprised, the way I am when I'm *reading* a book. Gardner's method is probably safer. The only potential risk is the writer's boredom with a foreseen plot, which can be offset by his anticipation of *how* it will be revealed. My way of working presents a more serious risk, of plunging recklessly ahead with a story that may eventually simply peter out and die. I've often thought that I'd end up writing a novel called *Nothing Happened*, and, in fact, I have a considerable backlog of false starts, of anywhere from twenty to two hundred pages long. But I'm thrifty, at least in one sense; I never *literally* throw out anything I've written, so I'm able to make narrative pen wipers and pot holders out of the scraps of unfinished material. I've discovered that it's possible to graft snippets and even long passages of failed stories and novels—after making some appropriate changes—onto other, more viable manuscripts.

Real life can be quite amorphous, and therefore terrifying at times. We know that we're going to die at the end of our mortal story, but we don't usually know when or how. And then there's all that other unpredictable stuff we have to go through first. Fiction, on the other hand, is contained and shapely. I think that many of us make up stories to help us deal with our fears of the boundless actual world. Writing is a way of mastering the unknown and the uncontrollable and establishing reason and order. Yet our fiction, like our lives, often suffers from a lack of structure. When the workshop writer defends his scrawny, half-formed story as a "slice of life," I'm inclined to say that a slice just doesn't fill me up, that what he's written only adds up to *notes* for a story.

It's very helpful to think in terms of a beginning, a middle, and an end. The opening of a story is crucial to the reader's continuing commitment to it. I view it as a kind of seduction, an invitation to come inside, like the spiel of a sideshow barker or the menu posted in a restaurant's window. Think of some of your favorite novels and the way they drew you in. The first time I read " 'Where's Papa going with that ax?' said Fern to her mother as they were setting the table for breakfast," my curiosity was as aroused as Fern's, although I already suspected that breakfast had something to do with the answer to her question. It's a perfect opening to a story—characters, dialogue, and a question that bears answering—yet it wasn't the only one that occurred to E. B. White when he began to write *Charlotte's Web.* In an early draft of the manuscript, he started with a description of the barnyard, material that he ultimately moved to a later chapter.

New writers tend to cram a lot of information into the very beginning of a piece, out of impatience to tell all or out of fear of losing the reader. I've read workshop manuscripts with ten or twelve characters introduced by name in the first paragraph, none of them memorably, and stories whose events are summarized right at the outset. In most instances, characters should enter a story as people enter one's life, in a natural progression. Events should evolve in a similar way, although fiction is usually much more selective than life and doesn't include everything that might happen. As children's author Jane Yolen says, "Plot signifies what happens in a story—and what does not." But "what does not" is sometimes present in an early draft of a manuscript and only extracted later, when the writer starts to feel confident in the basic framework of his story.

A good story or novel always has a solid structure, yet unlike formal poetry, it doesn't have to follow a set pattern. A story may open at its chronological beginning: "Henry was born in the town of M. in 19—" and then continue with an orderly sequence of events that ultimately lead to Henry's death. Or it might begin at the end, "Henry died in the town of S. in 19—," and then flash back to an earlier time (a technique often used in the movies). Nervier writers start right in the middle of a story and then flash forward and backward in turn. With a little practice, almost anyone can write a good first line with enough mystery and originality in it to hook the reader. The trick is in writing the second line, and all the ones after that. The middle of a story or novel, like the second act of a play or movie, is the hardest to carry off. It doesn't have the advantage of newness, as the beginning does, or the ending's impetus toward revelation and resolution. There are times when it takes real self-control not to skip ahead when reading the dull middle passages of a manuscript (or of a published book, for that matter). Of course all the parts of a story can't have the same energy or emotional weight, but nothing should seem like mere filler or connective tissue holding the highlights together. The movies can be particularly helpful to writers who have trouble segueing gracefully from one scene to another. In Westerns, for instance, when the cowboy leaves the saloon to head back to his ranch, we don't see him riding his horse for five or six miles; we simply fade out at the saloon or the hitching post and fade in again at the ranch. When I'm reading critically, I'll usually suggest deleting anything that doesn't either move the plot forward or illuminate the characters.

As a child, I often read the end of a book first, even the good ones, the equivalent of eating dessert at the start of a meal (which I also did). Like most kids, I wanted instant gratification; since then I've learned to wait for both my epiphanies and my ice cream. But there are occasions, after I've finished reading a student's or colleague's manuscript, when I still feel "hungry" (that slice-of-life syndrome again). Something's definitely missing, although I'm not always sure what it is. I've even looked around for additional pages I might have dropped. I'll ask myself if the story satisfies the writer's intentions. Was I promised something, explicitly or implicitly, that wasn't delivered?

After reading a draft of my first novel, my editor asked, "Where's the ending?" In a novel (coincidentally called *Ending*) about the terminal illness of a young husband and his wife's survival of that tragic event, I'd neglected to have him actually *die*.

"What a copout," the editor said, and of course he was right. And what a wasted opportunity to write a strong, dramatic scene. The final draft of the novel included that scene, as well as an earlier one in which the wife informs the husband of his awful prognosis. This, too, was written at my editor's suggestion. I'd originally had the doctor do the dirty work, offstage. If their marriage was as good as I'd shown it to be in the novel's early pages, the editor said, then they'd have to face this issue together. "But what will she say to him?" I asked. "And how will he take it? I mean, will he be cowardly or heroic?" To which the editor irritably replied, "How should *I* know? They're *your* characters." And of course he was right, again. They *were* my characters, in good times and in times of adversity. I knew them well enough after sharing about eight months and more than two hundred pages with them to figure it out for myself. I discovered in writing the scene that the husband was cowardly *and* heroic, as was his wife, and that they could not have been otherwise, given all the scenes that preceded this pivotal one, and helped to establish their distinctive temperaments. My editor's suggestions were not only psychologically sound but also good for the shape and texture of the novel. The rise and fall of a story's plot helps to keep the reader engaged.

Anatole Broyard used to suggest, when a story was too evenly paced or safely familiar, that the writer "radicalize" it: carry it to its furthest extremes. Most people quickly lose interest in a book that doesn't take some emotional and narrative risks, a book that reads like the electrocardiogram of a normal heart. An important point for workshop readers to consider is the *potential* of a piece of writing, and whether the writer has reached it or even really aimed for it. You have only to follow the daily newspaper account of a celebrated murder or child custody trial to see what I mean; something new and astonishing seems to turn up every day. Fiction has to hustle to keep up with that kind of convoluted and outrageous reality. But overreach can be another danger. If the boring manuscript you're reading is suddenly, joltingly enlivened by highly unlikely and unrelated events, you'd be obliged to protest. Some writers believe they can pull the reader back in by adding a little sex here and some gratuitous violence there, but good fiction isn't composed of fancy appliqués hastily stitched onto a dull background; it's a tapestry of all its components, seamlessly woven into a whole. A novel about middle-class suburban life can be quite radical and filled with surprises—comic and tragic—all within the realm of *possibility*, as in A. M. Homes's *Music for Torching*. She doesn't feel the need to have her characters abducted by aliens or devoured by cannibals in order to jazz up the plot. The wild turns it takes don't come from outer space but rather from what has already been given—"ordinary" human disaffection and despair—carried to its extremes.

Aristotle said, referring to drama, "The plot is the first essential and the soul of a tragedy; character comes second. . . . Men are what they are because of their characters, but it is in action that they find happiness or the reverse." But it may also be said (of drama and fiction) that the action is often dependent on the choices the characters make, and those choices dependent on who they are. Which is primary, character or action? It's like the old riddle of the chicken and the egg. My personal vote would be for character, but ideally character and plot are so intertwined and interdependent that we can't assign the major role to either one.

Maybe it's the influence of all those movies I've seen over the years, but I particularly enjoy reading and writing *scenes* in fiction, when we get to witness the story's events, rather than have them described to us. It's certainly an agreeable way for writers to avoid the habit of telling over showing. In a long descriptive or ruminative narrative sequence that's devoid of dramatic scenes, we become more aware of the writer pulling the characters' strings and more distanced from the characters themselves. It's like reading the synopsis of a novel instead of the real thing. Action and dialogue, those compatible components of scenes, not only reveal character as they move the plot along but also immerse the reader in the "reality" of the story. Strong scenes linked together by lean passages of straight narrative bring texture and a lively rhythm to the writing. A good storyteller translates the "moving pictures" inside her head into language that others can share.

Once, when my sister Ellie and I were teenagers, coming home from the movies on a bus, she began to tell me a juicy piece of gossip about a mutual friend. Right in the middle of the story, the woman sitting behind us leaned forward and tapped Ellie on the shoulder. "Could you hurry up and finish?" the woman said. "I've already gone past my stop." My sister, who doesn't write, is probably a born storyteller. She seems to know intuitively how to order events and dramatize scenes, and she provides just enough foreshadowing to hold the reader/eavesdropper captive until the denouement. A well-plotted novel, like a good piece of gossip, usually contains a modest amount of foreshadowing. Mary's habit of taking the shortcut home from work through a tough neighborhood alerts us to the possibility of danger. When she's finally mugged, we may be startled, but we don't feel as if we've been mugged, too, by the writer. Michael Cunningham's novel *The Hours* is presented in three sections; each is pleasurable to read on its own, but the three are only vaguely related to one another until near the end of the book, when they converge. There's some subtle foreshadowing, and even an inevitability about the dovetailing of these lives and events. Cunningham doesn't mask the connections, yet he takes his readers by surprise in the same way that life surprises us with its unexpected twists.

The heavy-handed writer is like the child who exclaims, "Watch out, Danny is hiding behind the door, and he's going to jump out and yell 'Boo!' " relieving his own anxiety, perhaps, while spoiling the surprise for everyone else. But the writer who deliberately withholds information in order to preserve the suspense of his story is cheating. If we're inside a character's head, we have to know what he's thinking that's relevant to the plot, unless, as in Jay McInerney's *Bright Lights, Big City*, he's repressing his darkest thoughts. Sometimes the writer sets down a clue that just leads the reader to a dead end. That sort of red herring is indicative of an amateur at work. As Chekhov said, "One must not put a loaded rifle on stage if no one is thinking of firing it." But this doesn't mean that everything has to be neatly tied together at the end, the way it usually is by the "tag" at the end of a television drama.

When someone in your workshop faults you for the unlikely coincidence that conveniently resolves your story, you will probably be tempted to say that coincidences happen all the time, which is true. Your wife's brother once dated your own first girlfriend, and you have the pictures to prove it! Those identical twins separated at birth really did show up at the same bar on the same day twenty years later—it was in all the newspapers! But we accept coincidences in life more readily than we do in fiction. The writer has to make the reader believe in the possibility, if not the probability, of his story's events. In Scott

Spencer's novel *Endless Love*, the hero and his estranged girl-friend's father converge unexpectedly in a city where neither lives, and their chance meeting results in a fatal accident. The reader (like the hero) is caught off guard, even stunned by this fluke, but not incredulous; it *might* have happened.

Flannery O'Connor said that people often pointed out to her that life in Georgia wasn't the way she depicted it, that escaped criminals didn't roam the roads exterminating whole families, nor did Bible salesmen prowl about looking for girls with wooden legs. They truly do, though, in her stories, where coincidences happen just as naturally. In "Everything That Rises Must Converge," a white woman, who's a racist, is a passenger on a bus when a black woman wearing an identical hat comes aboard. Does such comic and poetic justice ever really occur? Once again, it does, when the writing is so persuasive that art becomes life.

But I've seen workshop stories that weren't going anywhere suddenly resolved by an impossible coincidence, a last-minute injection of plot turn that doesn't save the patient or revive the reader's interest. This happens most often in manuscripts that depend too much on plot and not enough on character, the kind of story Trollope referred to as "the vehicle without the passengers." In the best stories plot and character coalesce to create narrative and emotional suspense, the dynamic synergy that kept Scheherazade alive, and that eavesdropping woman on my bus riding past her stop. In *Burning Down the House*, his book of essays on fiction, Charles Baxter says, "Stories bring characters together . . . mixed and matched, sometimes pushing them toward each other like chaperones who see to it that the diffident seventh graders in dancing class are suddenly, and against all expectations, in one another's arms."

When I poked my father awake during those bedtime stories to ask what happened next, it was Goldilocks herself I was interested in, not some hypothetical girl involved in an escalating situation with three bears. But if Goldilocks hadn't left the cozy and boring safety of her home to enter the woods, if she hadn't wandered into the bears' cottage and tasted their porridge and sat in their chairs and slept in their beds, I wouldn't have cared much about her, either.

This intuitive childhood response to a fairy tale has stayed with me throughout my adult life as a reader, writer, and teacher of fiction. In an analysis of workshop stories, I always consider the integration of character and plot, not just the success of either element. Focus sessions dealing with structure and/or character provide the opportunity to share ideas about achieving that integration.

11

The Long and the Short of It

Not that the story need be long, but it will take a long while to make it short.

—Henry David Thoreau

Writers and critics are always trying to define various writing forms and then differentiate between them. The novel and the short story come up frequently during this kind of debate, as if they're in competition with one another. Since manuscripts in both forms are presented in most fiction workshops, one of your group's focus sessions will probably deal with similar comparisons. Here are some of the questions that might arise:

- How can you tell whether you've begun to write (or read) a short story or a novel?

- Are there different ways of talking critically about stories and novels?
- How do you present a chapter of a novel (out of context) in the workshop?
- Is writing a short story a rehearsal for writing a novel?
- What *are* the major differences between the two forms?

The German critic-philosopher Walter Benjamin regarded the short story as an abbreviated novel. But Susanne Pari, who writes in both forms, maintains that they're as different as a love affair and a marriage. I'm not sure if she's referring to their respective longevity or level of bliss; perhaps both. Robert Olen Butler is more specific. "In a short story," he says, "there can be a number of connected incidents, but the ultimate focus is on a moment. In a novel there are a number of individual moments of clarity and insight, but ultimately the focus is on the causally connected chain of incidents."

I especially like John Cheever's take on the short story: "It's what you tell yourself in your dentist's office while you're waiting for an appointment." He sees it as an "appeasement of pain, in a very special sense, in a stuck ski lift, a sinking boat, a dentist's office, or a doctor's office—where we're waiting for a death warrant. Where you don't really have long enough for a novel, you do the short story." He concludes by saying, "I'm very sure that, at the very point of death, one tells oneself a short story—not a novel."

Short stories are sometimes likened to poems, broadening the equation. Tess Gallagher, who moves fluently between those two forms, says,

Short story and poem are close relatives when it comes to giving "the moment," and perhaps this is why there are

more poets who write stories than seem to write novels.
Story writing often allows some of the same strategies as
poetry—for instance, the use of epiphany, the use of
metaphor and simile, quickness or movement in time,
and the lyrical stripping down of narrative and detail to
essentials.

The short story enjoyed a renaissance with the publication
of collections by such gifted writers as Raymond Carver (who
also wrote poetry), Lorrie Moore, David Leavitt, and Anne Beattie. But talented, untried writers are often advised to get a novel
published first, in order to make a name for themselves. It
seems odd that in our fast-food culture, where instant gratification is primary, and where we wait impatiently for quick proce-
dures—at the ATM machine, for instance, or for that mocha
latte to go—the short story isn't in greater demand. Maybe the
ones we tell ourselves in the circumstances Cheever describes
satisfy our needs. Or maybe we don't have as urgent a sense of
our own mortality as he did.

Whenever I've presented a chapter of a novel-in-progress for
criticism in a workshop, someone invariably says she wants to
know more than I've told in that particular segment about a
character or a situation. But whatever seems to be missing is
often something I've intended to include in a *future* chapter.
"Just wait," I keep wanting to say, "the good stuff is coming
soon!" Pieces of a novel may offer their own small satisfactions,
but they don't fulfill a reader's desire for the whole picture. It's
like looking into a shard of mirror, seeing the reflection of just
your eyes or your feet—intriguing glimpses, maybe, but not the
composite of all your disparate elements (in effect, *you*).

Charles Dickens and Isaac Bashevis Singer both wrote serialized novels for newspapers. They knew how and where to break the narrative, so that their readers' interest and curiosity were only temporarily allayed, and how to pick it up again to summon those same readers back in. I think it's a good idea to write a long work as if it's going to be read serially. And workshop members who are analyzing individual chapters should, ideally, apply the patience and trust they use when reading novels published that way. But it's not so easy to do when the workshop chapters aren't submitted on a regular basis. Imagine your subscription to the newspaper going astray or losing the novel you're so avidly reading in the sofa cushions for a while. If several weeks or months have elapsed since the previous chapter of your novel was presented to the group, attaching a brief synopsis of it to the current manuscript will be helpful. Don't get carried away, though, by retelling everything in minute detail, and don't ever summarize what's going to happen next; let them want to know and wait to find out. Even when your readers are a little disoriented by the plot development or the characters, they should apply the same criteria for criticizing the writing itself (voice, language, etc.) to self-contained stories and to the chapters of a longer work. The reader may reasonably expect some changes to take place from chapter to chapter in a novel, even if they come in smaller increments than the evolution of emotions and events in a short story.

I used to believe that the short story was the writer's juvenilia and the novel her maturity. It was an honest mistake. Stories came to me fairly easily in the beginning—a first draft often represented a single hard-day's work—but writing a novel seemed like a formidable, even insurmountable, task. And when the stories first appeared in print, a few editors wrote to inquire if I had written a novel, which I interpreted as a question about my development as a writer: was I a grown-up yet? Since then I've heard (and readily agreed with) Raymond Carver's assessment: "One good short story is worth any number of bad novels." And after rereading his remarkable stories, and the stories of Anton Chekhov, John Cheever, Flannery O'Connor, Frank O'Connor, Eudora Welty, and Grace Paley, some of whom have also written novels, I view both forms as equally challenging and mature endeavors. As for the differences, I'm of the same mind as Robert Olen Butler: the short story might be said to highlight an event or situation and the novel to amplify it. Poe referred to the "single mood" of the short story and said that every sentence must contribute to it. The novel still takes much longer to write, and I believe that one can sustain a level of intensity throughout a short story that would wear out both the writer and the reader in the course of a novel.

Talking about process, Stanley Elkin said that he usually had an entire short story in view when he began to write it, but that he was "incapable of long-distance plotting," leaving the events of his novels to be discovered during the writing itself. In 1978, Joyce Carol Oates noted that "a short story is bliss to write set beside a novel of even ordinary proportions." But then she went on to say that she wasn't sure why, but she hadn't been writing much short fiction lately. And Rosellen Brown notes, wistfully: "I used to be a writer, but now I'm a *novelist.*" I know what she means; the saddest thing for me is that I can't seem to switch back and forth between the short story and the novel with ease. After I wrote my first novel, I began to think and dream in broader, more novelistic terms, and I've only written and published a few short stories since then. I miss writing them, but at least I still have the pleasure of reading other people's stories.

Sometimes works of fiction transcend conventional classification, although people still try to categorize them. Very long stories (or short novels) like Katherine Anne Porter's *Pale Horse, Pale Rider* and Joseph Conrad's *Heart of Darkness* are referred to as "novellas." The manuscript of Amy Tan's *The Joy Luck Club* was submitted to editor Faith Sale as a group of discrete stories. Tan was surprised by some of the similarities and connections Sale saw in them. Together, they arranged the stories in sections related to the four families they portrayed. One story that seemed very different from the others was dropped, and stronger links were made among the remaining ones. Both Amy Tan and Faith Sale still thought of them as an assemblage of stories, but most of the reading and critical public perceived them, collectively, as a well-made novel.

In Louise Erdrich's introduction to the *Best American Short Stories of 1993*, which she edited, she wrote, "The best short stories contain novels. Either they are densely plotted, with each line an insight, or they distill emotions that could easily have spread on for pages, chapters." So one can perceive the story not as a shorter version of a novel (with some essential elements left out), but as a compression of those elements, the way a poem often is. Sometimes I'll start out with the intention of writing a short story, based, perhaps, on a single imagined or reimagined incident, involving one or two characters, and I'll discover that it needs to be expanded, to be made not just longer, but also "wider" and more leisurely told, as well. I'll feel the need to reveal more about the history of the main characters, and other, seemingly minor, figures will insist on their fair share of attention, too. The waiter who steps momentarily from the shadows to serve coffee to the hero, or the priest who hears his confession refuse to recede into obscurity. They, too, have lives that demand examination and explication. Don DeLillo's novel *Underworld* artfully demonstrates the way this happens, by following what seem like supporting characters into their own private worlds.

When I'm writing what I believe is a longish, complex story, it sometimes breaks itself up into episodes that lead toward a denouement somewhere in the unknown distance, which I'll feel driven to reach. In the meantime, subplots arise and insert themselves into the narrative, and characters invite other characters in without even consulting me. When these things happen, I know I've begun to write a novel, something that can't be written (or read) in a single sitting. The reverse occurs when I set out to write a novel and find that I'm simply padding a short story with extraneous characters and situations in order to fulfill my original plan.

Charles Baxter offers two hypotheses about the story and the novel:

> *Obvious point: Short stories end before novels do and therefore have a more critical relation to the immediacy of closure and what might constitute it. Arguable point: Characters in short stories, unlike the characters in novels, do not, as a rule, make long-term plans. They tend instead, to be creatures of impulse.*

The first point *is* fairly obvious, and the second quite provocative. It makes me wonder whether I and the people I know would be more likely (because of our individual temperaments) to be characters in long or short fiction. Maybe we'd all change with age and experience and move back and forth between the two forms. But there are no hard-and-fast rules. A novel can take place in the span of a single day, as do *Mrs. Dalloway* and *Ulysses*, and a short story can track its characters over a long period of time, forcing them to consider the future, as several of Alice Munro's stories do.

Once, at an artist's colony, I began to write what I thought was going to be a novel, based on a single incident and a handful of characters. After about a week, I started to see it more as a short story, and I proceeded to contract and condense its various elements. A few days later, I realized the story wasn't working, either; it, too, was being artificially expanded to fit the form. Then I tinkered with the notion of a narrative poem, something I'd tried to write in the past without much success. That effort failed, as well, so I scrapped the whole thing and began writing something else. I was reminded of my soapstone sculpture, and of my young children, who used to move the food they didn't like around on their plates until it "disappeared."

My novel *In the Flesh* began as a series of short stories about the same characters, of whom I'd grown quite fond (although they had been living in my head so long I believed they should pay rent!). The stories appeared to have a forward trajectory, and someone in my workshop suggested that I turn them into a novel. I'd published my first novel by then and was suffering from that dreaded second-novel syndrome—was the first book just a fluke? Did I have another one in me?—so I welcomed the idea. The challenge was to put the stories together so that they wouldn't look as if they'd been connected by mere will and a little spit. Several of them had already been published, which seemed to set them in stone, and I had difficulty violating their individual integrity for the larger good. People in my workshop remembered the stories, and when I began to present what I now called "chapters," a few of them noticed how loath I was to make changes. One man sensibly advised that every chapter not end in an epiphany. Another suggested that material I was reluctant to cut from a particular story might be set aside and used elsewhere in the novel, which is good advice about deletions at any time. It gives the writer courage to let go. Someone else said that writing a few new scenes would free me from my commitment to some of the old ones. Little by little, my fellow writers helped me to shape those separate entities into a reasonable whole. I don't think I could have done it alone.

Ann Beattie once needed similar support, as she revealed in an interview.

> Early on, I had about 75 pages of a story I couldn't conclude. I asked for advice, and was told by a friend who's always read my work, "Just put chapter 1 on page 1, and chapter 2 on page 15." So I did, and it became Chilly Scenes [her first novel, Chilly Scenes of Winter].

Beattie cites another major difference between the two forms, besides length, mood, and event. "You have to use language differently," she says. "Mention an image twice in a story, and you can usually count on it to reverberate; mention it twice in a novel, and it's probably lost in the long text." Edith Konecky says that you have more freedom in the novel, and Lynda Schor finds the story, with its expansion of a moment, the more natural form for herself, because of her interest in short spans of time.

More than one story can be told within the space of a single novel, as they are in *The World According to Garp* and John Gardner's *October Light*, and the possibility of a novel may be contained within the confines of a short story. Randall Jarrell says that a story (and I believe he's speaking generically of fiction) is a sort of dream, in that it satisfies wishes. Perhaps the short story can be compared to a catnap or a reverie and the novel to a long slumber and its attendant sustained dream.

When asked how she decides whether she's going to write a short story or a novel, Joanne Greenberg said:

> *It decides. You get a package in the mail which is a kit.*
> *But the kit doesn't have any labels on it. Is it the bird*
> *house or is it the cathedral? Well, you open the kit. This*
> *looks like the bird house kit. Alright. But what's that big*
> *arch doing in the bird house kit? Maybe it's the cathedral*
> *kit. What are all these pieces doing here? There are*
> *too many pieces for the bird house kit. I think it's the*
> *cathedral.*

I quite agree, although I use a different metaphor (of course!) to make the same point. One of the astounding things about goldfish is that they will grow to suit their environment. Move a little one from his domestic bowl to a capacious pond and he'll expand accordingly. The amazing thing about fiction is that it seems to find its own size and form, too. But the most essential fact about short stories and novels is that they're all *written*, and, putting the time element aside, require the same diligent and passionate attention to language, character, and truth. The principles of good writing are of equal consequence in either form.

12

The Voice Behind
the Screen

*Dorothy asked, "Where are you?" "I am everywhere," an-
swered the Voice, "but to the eyes of common mortals I
am invisible."*

—L. FRANK BAUM, *THE WONDERFUL WIZARD OF OZ*

In the sixth grade, my classmates and I were tested by our
music teacher, Mr. Dipietro, for a place in the school chorus.
Like all children, I enjoyed singing; emotionally high-pitched, I
assumed I'd be declared a soprano. For the audition each of us
was asked to render, out of season, a few bars of "Adeste Fi-
delis." When my turn came, I managed to croak out only a single
note, the opening "O" of the carol, before Mr. Dipietro held up
his hand like a traffic cop and announced that I was a listener.
One of my continuing disappointments is that I can't sing well. If
someone near me is singing harmony, I sing harmony; if he's
singing melody, so do I. And I keep changing keys without knowing I'm doing it. My family won't even let me sing rounds with

them in the car because I throw everyone else off. Maybe I really became a writer in order to have more of a "voice" in things.

Essayist and poet Nancy Mairs says that she's frequently asked, by those interested in writing, "How did you find your voice?" The locution troubles her because it suggests something was missing or lost. She would rephrase the question and have it asked of her *voice*, not herself: "How did you find (devise, invent, contrive) your Nancy?" But the question of voice, no matter how it's put, persists. It's frequently cited in book reviews, where the writer is praised for having a unique, compelling, compassionate, or persuasive voice, or it is damned for sounding affected or unconvincing. And in college catalogues the goal of a fiction workshop is sometimes stated as "the discovery and development of each member's individual voice." But what does that really mean?

The *Random House College Dictionary* offers seventeen definitions of the word *voice*. Among them: "the sound or sounds uttered through the mouth of living creatures, especially of human beings, in speaking, shouting, singing, etc.; a range of such sounds distinctive to one person; an expressed will or desire: i.e., the voice of the people; a quality that seem to proceed from a will or personality; to give utterance or expression to, to declare; proclaim." Any or all of these definitions seem close to the spirit and meaning of the writing voice, which makes me contemplate how one "discovers and develops" (or devises, invents, contrives) one's own. Perhaps the best place to begin is at the beginning, with our earliest infant noises.

According to the Swiss psychologist-philosopher Jean Piaget, all thinking and speaking during the first seven years of life is egocentric. The child isn't concerned about having an audience for his babble; he can't keep secrets, but he's only telling them to himself. After seven, Piaget tells us, socialization of speech sets in. Some secrets are kept, some lies are told. The audience starts to matter, and verbal communication really begins. I'd like to suggest that one's writing voice is a combination of egocentric speech—talking to oneself for comfort and pleasure—and socialized speech—reaching out to others for a response. But while it would seem to develop naturally, out of speech and will and personality, a comfortable writing voice often remains elusive, presenting more problems to the novice than almost any other aspect of his craft.

Forget that your mother used to tell you not to begin too many sentences with the word "I" when you were writing a thank-you letter to your aunt, that it made you sound self-centered. (What child isn't?) A first-person narrative is probably the easiest approach to a first work of fiction, because it's so much like speaking directly to someone you know. Maybe that's one of the reasons we feel such affection and sympathy for Holden Caulfield and for Dickens's Pip. Like the present tense, the first person has the advantages of intimacy and intensity. It can become claustrophobic or unintentionally solipsistic, though (your mother was partially right), especially when supporting characters have little to say or do in the narrative, or the "I" character's voice isn't very lively or persuasive. When a drowning character in someone's workshop story commented on her own gorgeous, tawny hair floating out behind her like a mermaid's, I had trouble believing in her plight, not to mention her ability to see behind herself. And her vanity—given the circumstances—was exasperating. I mean, she wasn't just having a *good* hair day. A character who whines throughout her narrative, and never seems to gain any insight from her experiences, is equally unsympathetic. As translator Elizabeth Hanson said in the *New York Times Book Review*, "Reading a novel with a first-person narrator is a bit like strapping yourself into a seat next to a voluble stranger for a transcontinental flight. You hope your seatmate has an interesting story to tell, or at least an interesting way to tell a dull one."

The lesser-used second person (with which the narrator addresses the reader or another character as "you") is also intimate, but more frequently in danger of becoming precious or tedious. For its successful employment, read *Lady Susan*, Jane Austen's epistolary novel; or *Bright Lights, Big City*, in which the "you" addressed is the narrator himself, seeking some emotional detachment from his own painful story. And many of us still delight in the sudden confidentiality of Jane Eyre's "Reader, I married him."

The third person may be very broad: inside everyone's head, or at least the major players' and the writer's, or limited to only one or two characters' points of view. It reminds me of the overview you get from an airplane flying at varying altitudes. The higher you go, the farther you see, but perhaps with less clarity. In any case, the use of the third person might distance the reader somewhat, but it generally offers a wider spectrum of the circumstances and events than the first or second person: at least you'll get more than *one* side of the story, opening up its possibilities.

The story itself often dictates the choice of usage. The first-person narration of Arthur Golden's *Memoir of a Geisha*, a very private yet revealing story told within a larger social and histor-

ical framework, seems absolutely right. Compelled by the female voice of the narrator, one easily forgets or doesn't really
care that the writer is a man. The same is true of Brian Moore's
I Am Mary Dunne. Flaubert might have written *Madame Bovary*
in the first person, too, limiting it to Emma's shallow longings,
her roller-coaster ride of ecstasy and despair. But, as Mary Mc-
Carthy notes in her Foreword to one edition of the novel, "Without Charles [Bovary], Emma would be the moral void that her
fatuous conversation and actions disclose. Charles, in a novelistic sense, is her redeemer. To her husband she is sacred, and
this profound and simple emotion is contagious." In a similar
vein, Daniel Stern urges writers to "create another character
against which your main character can measure, test and define
him- or herself."

A novel by Joan Chase called *During the Reign of the Queen
of Persia* is told in the multiple voices of the four central characters, two sets of young sisters (who are cousins) on a farm in
northern Ohio. Chase has them speak as "we" in the book and
yet manages not to blend their voices into a single chorus (like
the Supremes, with herself as Diana Ross). She avoids that by
making sharp, separate observations of and by Celia, Jenny,
Katie, and Anne. The common denominators of family and adolescence don't interfere with the individuality of each character.
But we also see them as a strong unit. It's done in this voice:
"There were four of us then, two his daughters, two his nieces,
all of us born within two years of each other. . . ." And then in
this voice: "One early spring morning when Celia was fourteen
and the rest of us girls thirteen or nearly so . . . ." The book won
the PEN/Hemingway Award in 1983, and the citation read, in
part, "By allowing her story to unfold according to its natural

rhythms, Joan Chase has created a brilliant pattern of connecting lives." It's as easy and as complicated as that.

Choosing the voice with which to tell a particular story may be the fiction writer's most important decision. Sometimes, though, the voice comes first, entering the writer's consciousness with just an enigmatic sentence or two. I've heard that poets often begin their poems this way, not sure of what will follow. When that happens to me, when I hear a voice (or two) in my head, I write the sentences down and then wait for more, hoping the characters will eventually tell me their whole story. It's chancy, though—characters can be so perverse—and I often wish there was an exact formula for creating a fictional voice. Unfortunately, the process remains as abstract as one of my mother's recipes. She was a terrific cook who could never have written a cookbook. "Take a handful of flour," she'd instruct. But whose hand was she talking about? Hers was so small compared to mine. "Touch the dough," she'd say. "It should feel springy—like *this*." When it didn't work out, when my dough sank rather than sprung, she'd suggest I start anew, with a fresh "handful" of flour. I think she was trying to tell me to rely on intuition and practice—good advice for a writer, too.

Virginia Woolf said that the best writing is androgynous, and Rita Mae Brown suggests all writers be bisexual, at least in their imagination. Renoir, on the other hand, is said to have boasted that he painted with his penis, which creates a weirdly comical mind picture for me (especially when I think of painters cleaning their brushes in turpentine). Of course it's only a metaphorical reference that has to do with his maleness addressing the female form.

There is always an aspect of self in one's writing voice. Nancy Mairs expresses this nicely when she refers to "the auto-biographical pitch and timbre distinguishing this voice that utters me." I believe that we bring every part of our innate being and experience to every kind of artistic expression, that we can't and shouldn't deny such aspects as our gender, sexual preference, skin color, or nationality, and that neither Woolf nor Brown are really suggesting we do so. Rather, they're asking that we not be *limited* by destiny, biological or otherwise. One of Stanley Elkin's characters defines morality as "the awareness of others." The "bisexual" writer is one who allows herself to imagine fully the mysterious "otherness" of everyone else—male or female—through generosity of vision and with utter freedom of expression. To develop an interesting writing voice, to avoid suffocating and primarily self-referential writing, you must be able to intuit or conjure up what you are *not*, to incorporate, in a sense, the entire world around you. Jane Smiley did it in her novel *The Greenlanders*, about a remote civilization during the fourteenth century. And Ethan Canin did it, as a young writing student, by successfully imagining the inner lives of much older characters.

In one of Flaubert's astonishing letters to his lover, Louise Colet, he wrote, in the rhapsodic aftermath of a good writing day:

> *What a delicious thing writing is—not to be you anymore,*
> *but to move through the whole universe you're talking*
> *about. Take me today, for instance; I was a man and*
> *woman, lover and mistress; I went riding in a forest on*
> *a fall afternoon beneath the yellow leaves, and I was the*

> *horses, the leaves, the wind, the words he and she spoke,*
> *and the red sun beating on their half-closed eyelids which*
> *were already heavy with passion.*

But what confidence that takes! How can the writer possibly speak for everyone and everything within the confines of his story? Here's where my old music teacher comes in handy. His crushing pronouncement of me as a listener may have also been a kind of blessing. Writers must take their role as listeners to heart, if only to capture someone else's rhythms and tone, or the vibrations that precede the voice of a new story. Eudora Welty says, "Listening children know stories are *there*. When their elders sit and begin, children are just waiting and hoping for one to come out, like a mouse from its hole." And in an interview, Ralph Ellison said, "I think basically my instinctive approach to writing is through sound . . . one of the things I work for is to make a line of prose sound right, or for a bit of dialogue to fall on the page in the way I hear it, aurally, in my mind." Another kind of listening is described by psychoanalyst Theodor Reik:

> *It can be demonstrated that the analyst, like his patient,*
> *knows things without knowing that he knows them. The*
> *voice that speaks in him, speaks low, but he who listens*
> *with a third ear hears also what is expressed noiselessly,*
> *what is said pianissimo.*

A parallel can easily be made between the analyst and patient and the listening writer at work. Nabokov reports his own, idiosyncratic case of what he calls "colored hearing." In *Speak, Memory* he says, "The long *a* of the English alphabet has for me the tint of weathered wood, but a French *a* evokes polished ebony. This black group also includes hard *a* (vulcanized rubber) and *r* (a sooty rag being ripped) . . ." An oddly original perception that surely contributes to his unique writing voice.

As a child I used to think it strange that my parents enjoyed listening to tap dancing on the radio. I could appreciate the appeal of radio plays and soap operas. I, myself, was addicted to "Let's Pretend," and the many voices of Irene Wicker, the Singing Lady. This was, after all, in the olden days—before the advent of television—when you had to picture things. But *tap dancing?* Now I believe I understand how that infectious beat—that sent my mother's fingers dancing across the kitchen table, my father's shoe keeping time on the linoleum—was a springboard for the imagination and enabled them to "see," as they listened, top hats and tails, the glittering, polished dance floor, and the intricate acrobatics of the performers. The dancers' collective "voice" was in the rhythm of their tapping feet. The rhythm of written language, which is only one component of the writing voice, can make an impressive illusion, too.

In "The Enormous Radio," an early short story by John Cheever, he comes up with an ingenious device for eavesdropping, a radio in someone's apartment that happens to pick up and transmit the sounds from several other apartments in the same building. At first the overheard conversation seems to be an innocuous form of indoor entertainment. " 'Have you seen my garters?' a man asked. 'Button me up,' a woman said. 'Have you seen my garters?' the man said again. 'Just button me up and I'll find your garters,' the woman said." A nursemaid reads aloud to her little charges: "Lady Jingley! Lady Jingley! Sitting where the pumpkins blow, will you come and be my wife, said the Younghy-

Bonghy-Bo. . . ." Then the tension of commonplace life begins to build. " 'I don't want to go to school,' a child screamed. . . . 'You will go to school,' an enraged woman said. 'We paid eight hundred dollars to get you into that school and you'll go if it kills you.' " The sense of desperation continues to grow. It turns out that the handyman is having an affair with a woman in the building. Another man beats his wife during an argument. The elevator man has tuberculosis. Someone has heart trouble and someone else is losing his job. The entire spectrum of human despair is revealed through these overheard conversations, and the married couple who overhear them are ultimately forced to face their own troubled existence, their own version of misery. This brilliant little story might serve as a paradigm of the purposes of fiction, to amuse and inform the reader, but to also help illuminate his own life. And it's not done with mirrors, or with some other kind of backstage sleight of hand. It's done with the sound of several minor voices, orchestrated into a commanding chorus.

Robert Frost wrote in a letter: "The ear does it. The ear is the only true writer and the only true reader." And in one of his essays on having AIDS, Harold Brodkey refers to his impending death as a passage "toward one's absorption into the dance of particles and inaudibility."

Inaudibility—such a sad word. So listen up. Don't waste that next bus trip, that next visit to the laundromat, the supermarket, or the local diner. Listen to your children, your neighbors, even your radio, then write it all down. And, once again (I can't really say it too often), read your work aloud and listen for those particular sounds, those rhythms, those accents that have become, mysteriously, your writing voice. Keep listening to your workshop colleagues, too, taking note of their separate and distinctive writing voices, and the common language of criticism you've developed. Most of all, listen to the voices of your characters as they try to tell you their story. Even though I still regret not being allowed to sing in my elementary school chorus, I'm glad I became such a dedicated listener. Thanks, Mr. Dipietro!

13

Knock, Knock.
Who's There?

Give people human beings, not yourself.

—ANTON CHEKHOV

It's late at night and you're lying in bed, reading or dreaming, when there's an urgent knocking at the door. Who can it be at this hour? You're not expecting company, and it's much too late for the Avon lady to be calling. When you go to the door, a total stranger is standing there—a large, disheveled woman, breathing heavily and burdened with shopping bags. "Yes?" you ask suspiciously through the barely opened door, but she pushes past you and comes inside. Before you can demand to know her business, she comes uncomfortably close and whispers hotly, "Listen, you lucky dog, I've come to tell you the story of my life." This is only one of many ways that fictional characters are conceived.

Stendahl, in a letter to Balzac, wrote, "I take a being whom I have known, and say to myself; with the same habits, contracted in the art of going every morning 'in pursuit of pleasure,' what would he do if he had more intelligence?" Samuel Richardson explained, "Hence sprung Pamela," and Dickens said, "I thought of Mr. Pickwick," as if he were recalling someone he knew. Both Dickens's and Richardson's statements preserve the mystery of artistic creation, as if the birth of literary characters takes place during a kind of twilight sleep from which the writer emerges refreshed and stimulated, and without memory of conception, gestation, or labor. It's been said, in keeping with the childbirth analogy, that at the moment of inspiration something leaves you. But Flaubert insisted, "It is something that enters into you."

During one of your group's discussions, you'll probably discover that some of you work primarily from ideas and then look around, like talent scouts, for suitable actors to play out the drama, while others (like me) subscribe to the "characters first" school of fiction, and Flaubert's notion of being invaded by them. At the risk of sounding like Joan of Arc, I hear my characters' voices first, usually with a single sentence: "I am bigger than life." "What smells like that?" "The way it was, I didn't love anybody." If they keep talking, I keep listening. The childhood companionship of several imaginary friends was probably good training for a future fiction writer. I've heard other writers speak about visual stimuli, of seeing a man or woman whose facial expression, posture, or merest gesture suggests a mood, a series of responsive gestures, a story. Perhaps the story lay buried in its author's unconscious for years, waiting to be unearthed one day by some physical cue. In the discussion of the (successful or unsuccessful) rendering of character in someone's workshop story, it might be instructive to ask the writer—when it's his turn to speak—how the characters were conceived. You're likely to find that those characters purported to be taken "directly" from life, without artistic alteration or elaboration, are usually less convincing than those that are inspired by the composite qualities of several people, or completely invented.

For me, the most satisfying novels are character driven, but fictional characters, like real people, can't live in a moral void. The events of their lives must challenge them to make choices, and those choices will help to define them. In Dickens's *A Tale of Two Cities*, the wastrel lawyer, Sidney Carton, finally redeems himself by sacrificing his very life for love. Sethe, the escaped slave in Toni Morrison's *Beloved*, risks death and more to achieve freedom. And the young soldier-hero of Stephen Crane's *The Red Badge of Courage* overcomes his panic in battle and goes on to lead a daring military charge.

Yet heroism on such a grand scale isn't always called for. One of the most beautifully realized characters in contemporary fiction is Evan Connell's antiheroine Mrs. Bridge, who simply lives a life of quiet desperation. Her passivity, or her choice *not* to act when she clearly should, reveals her not as stupid or evil, but as timid and repressed. The opening line of *Mrs. Bridge*—"Her first name was India—she was never able to get used to it"—attests to an early denial of her potential self: a unique and interesting woman. Indeed, she wonders if her parents had another child in mind when they named her, and she often thinks of asking them but never gets around to it. That, in summary, is the story of her life. The title of the book, *her* title in her consummate role as Mr. Bridge's wife, becomes her true identity.

Mrs. Bridge's dependency on her husband increases over the many years of their marriage, as she submits to his will on matters as diverse as politics, psychotherapy, and automobiles. Widowed by the end of the book, she's still driving one of the inappropriately oversize Lincolns Mr. Bridge purchased for her. It's in the car, symbolically stalled, that she finds herself trapped in the final pages, half in and half out of her garage, on a snowy morning, calling futilely, "Hello? Hello out there?" Several of novelist Richard Yates's characters suffer from a similar fatal apathy or wrongheadedness. Hampered by unhappy childhoods, malignant envy, and existential dread, they seem incapable of making judicious decisions about their own lives. It takes a dark vision and a lot of courage to begin a novel with "Neither of the Grimes sisters would have a happy life" as Yates does in *Easter Parade*. Connell's and Yates's considerable accomplishment is to make their patently self-destructive characters so tenderly real and sympathetic.

Raymond Carver remarked, about an early draft of Tess Gallagher's story "Girls," "Your characters are too nice. Make one of them a little less so and the tension will improve." She says, "In the next draft I made the daughter more eccentric and the whole story perked up." The legendary editor Maxwell Perkins once observed, "The trouble with American writing today is that there aren't enough rascals." And Charles Baxter says that fictional characters "are under no obligation to be good; they only have to be interesting." Sometimes out-and-out villainy is as interesting as heroism or antiheroism. Fictional villains (or rascals) who add tension and drama to a story can be as intriguing as the good guys, and often more so. We remember Iago as much as we do Othello, and Scrooge more than

Tiny Tim. Even Hannibal (the Cannibal) Lecter stays in the mind longer than FBI agent Clarice Starling (I had to look up her name, but not his).

In your workshop, you're bound to ask from time to time if a character in someone's story is likable, if there's anyone to root for. You might also ask if there's anyone *un*likable in the story, for the sake of that dramatic tension. But always remember that evildoers, like heroes, must be given proper dimension and a fair share of the action if they're to come to life. A few simple human gestures or observations can be enough to make even someone unsavory complex and real: the way his forehead moves when he chews, his habit of knocking on wood, and his imagining that he sees the figure of an angel in the stains on his bedroom ceiling. I heard a perfect sentence about a flawed but complex character in a workshop recently: "He tried to smile, but it didn't reach his eyes."

In his book *On Becoming a Novelist*, John Gardner writes,

> *What chiefly astonishes us in the work of this highest class of novelists—Tolstoy, Dostoevsky, Mann, Faulkner— is the writer's gift for rendering the precise observations and feelings of a wide variety of characters, even entering the minds (in Tolstoy's case) of animals. The beginning novelist who has the gift for inhabiting other lives has perhaps the best chance for success.*

But when I was a beginning novelist, someone in my workshop faulted my heroine for being "*too* damned observant. She's so busy noticing everything," my critic grumbled. "When does she *live*?" I could have argued that observing is a *way* of living, and I probably did, when it was my turn to speak. But it's a pointless defense if the heroine doesn't come to life for the reader. When a character is elusive, the complaints aren't always that specific. Someone might simply say, "I don't feel as if I know her," or, "I just can't *picture* her." It's helpful to have a few visual clues, to know if someone is tall or short, wall-eyed or bald, but it's merely distracting to be told that a character is 5'11½" tall and weighs 165 pounds. Certain aspects of his appearance may tell us something about his self-esteem, his sense of style, or his state of mind, but they're hardly ever a complete revelation of his personality. Both Richard Nixon and John Travolta, for instance, could be described as having dark hair and prominent jaws. Still, if a description is especially distinctive, it can become a strong component of the character's identity. The elderly heroine of British novelist Elizabeth Taylor's *Mrs. Palfrey at the Claremont* is easily evoked for me by this single line: "She would have made a distinguished-looking man and, sometimes, wearing evening dress, looked as Lord Louis Mountbatten might in drag."

In Anatole Broyard's remarkable short story "What the Cystoscope Said," the intellectual narrator doesn't really know his laborer father on any deep level. Instead, the son keeps an affectionate but supercilious distance. This occurs to him only after his father becomes seriously ill and the son must transport the toolbox his father had carried with such apparent ease for so many years.

> *The box was about two and a half feet long, eighteen inches wide, and six inches thick. It was made of plywood, stained mahogany, with metal-reinforced corners, and it held a surprising number of tools, because they were all ingeniously fitted into special slots. Although, as I said, I'd*

seen the box all my life, I'd never picked it up. I would no
more have picked it up than I would have picked up my
mother, as my father sometimes playfully did.

How interesting that the description of the toolbox is far more
scrupulous than any physical description of its owner, whose
terrible death is the focus of the story. As it turns out, the box is
stunningly heavy and unwieldy; the son, more than thirty years
younger than his father and much taller and heavier, can barely
heft it. This artifact of his father's long, laboring life, a life the
son had hardly contemplated before, seems now belatedly to define the man. The narrator of Broyard's story, in his ardent intellectual pursuits, has neglected the life of the body. Only the
approaching death of his father forces him to consider the physical and the metaphysical side by side.

Names, which are often the first things we learn about each
other in life, are another surprisingly important identifying feature of fictional characters. Mrs. Bridge denies the exotic possibilities of "India," and Mrs. Palfrey keeps her dignified distance
as she descends into the abyss of long widowhood and a lonely
old age. When we christen our characters, we have an advantage over Mrs. Bridge's parents, or any parents of a newborn
child: we already know a good deal about the personality and
the fate of the one we're naming. Think of all the little Amys,
Jos, Megs, and Beths out there who struggle all their lives to
live up to their namesakes. I was named for a fictional character
myself, one Hilma Tree, a voluptuous dairy maid in a Frank Nor-
ris novel, and I could never cut it on either count. Some of the
names we use in fiction are prompted by people we know, a Jen-
nifer or Michael we either love or despise. There are obvious
dangers in this practice, like lawsuits and hurt feelings. (I'd be

particularly wary of naming characters after fellow workshop members, no matter how flattering or playful you think you're being; the critique of the story will not be objective!)

I named a teenage couple in one of my juvenile novels after my nephew and his then main squeeze and, of course, by the time the book was published, they'd broken up. My daughter Meg (her real name is Margaret and she was *not* named for one of the Little Women), has five friends named Lisa, and when she called one of her fictional heroines Lisa, each of her same-named friends was certain she was the inspiration for the character. A novelist I know refers to the obituaries to find appropriate names for her characters, in a kind of literary reincarnation. John O'Hara used the telephone directory—another reason, besides crank calls, to keep oneself unlisted.

We have to remember that our main characters' names will probably be among the most frequently repeated words in our work. You might try saying a name aloud a few times just to hear how it sounds. Is Butch Manly too broad a label for your intrepid hero or too ironic for a timid soul? Would calling someone Penelope Annabelle Goldshreiber wear out the reader and distract from the character herself, or would it give her the antic distinction she so desperately needs? Writers often change the names of their characters in mid-novel. Scarlett O'Hara began her fictional life as Pansy, which is hard to imagine now that we know her as the brazen schemer she is. In the early drafts of some workshop manuscripts you may find confusing references to the same people under various aliases, until the writer makes up his mind. A name that "takes" right from the beginning is a good sign, I think, about your assured sense of the named. The British novelist David Lodge says, "One may hesitate and agonize about the choice of a name, but once made, it becomes inseparable from the character." When I began writing my novel *Hearts*, I knew that there were going to be two main female characters who are closely, if not harmoniously, connected, and I didn't want them to have confusing or interchangeable names. Anna and Hanna, to use an absurd example, definitely wouldn't have worked. Mary and May would have presented similar problems (especially to the typesetter). I'm not sure why, but the young stepmother in the story became "Linda" immediately; the name simply came to me as soon as I imagined her. It has a cheery sound, I think, and my Linda is doggedly upbeat, against all odds. In retrospect, I wonder if the popular Spanish song "*Linda Mujer*" (Pretty Woman) was in the back of my mind, tucked away there to be used later. In *Tunnel of Love*, the sequel to *Hearts*, Linda falls in love with a Hispanic man who calls her "*Linda Mujer*."

Linda's stepdaughter became "Robin" after I considered and rejected a few other popular contemporary names, like Stephanie and Michelle. Maybe Robin is an allusion to the bird; my character *is* in flight, from both her home and her emotions. I knew that the two names, Linda and Robin, would often appear together, and I wanted them to be appreciably different from one another, yet euphonius in tandem. I worried about the monotony of their having two syllables each, but having one end in a vowel and the other in a consonant seemed to help. While not typical, their names were still in keeping with the naming trends of their generations. In *Tunnel of Love*, Linda has her own biological child, whom she calls Phoebe, after her late mother. I named her after Holden Caulfield's little sister in *The Catcher in the Rye* (which Linda hadn't read). It didn't occur to me that Phoebe, like Robin, was the name of a bird, until I was almost through with the first draft of the manuscript. In the second draft, I let Robin make this discovery herself, and it helps to affirm the bond she's already made with her new half-sister.

To "know" a character is to perceive the essence of her being without having to read a complete FBI file on her. But uncertain writers may want to keep such extensive files on their characters in an effort to understand and deepen them. Here are a few questions you might ask yourself:

- Is this character religious?
- If a close friend committed a serious crime, would she turn her in?
- How would she vote in a national election?
- Does she have peculiar eating or sleeping habits?
- Can she speak more than one language?

Carefully considering these questions doesn't mean that the content of their answers must enter the story or novel. They're for the *writer's* edification, not the reader's. We don't have to see the character go to church, the police station, or the polls, and it isn't necessary to witness her secret bouts of bulimia or hear her exclaim in Spanish or French. If a character is presented as an obsessive-compulsive personality, the kind who squares off magazines against the edge of a table and always counts the steps as he enters a building, we may be spared his years on an analyst's couch. But it might benefit the *writer* to know that, as a child, this person was toilet trained with a gun, and that years after the end of the novel, his wife will leave him for a man whose socks and shorts litter the bedroom floor. Knowing as much about a character as possible allows the writer to sort through the details with confidence and present only those that are relevant to the story.

In addition to their names and personalities, most characters, like the rest of us, also have jobs of one kind or another. In *Hearts*, Linda teaches social dancing at a studio, something I simply *knew* about her, the way I knew her name. Endowing her with physical grace helps to make up for her lack of social grace and self-esteem. And because she has a variety of clients (some of them quite bizarre), her job provides the material for several diverse scenes. One of my main characters in another novel, *In the Palomar Arms*, is an elderly man about to enter a nursing home. I knew quite a bit about his circumstances at the outset. He was widowed, retired, and lived happily with his married daughter and grandchildren. What I didn't know was the infirmity that was forcing him into institutional care, and the profession he'd once practiced. I decided that Parkinson's disease would be his medical problem; a neighbor had suffered from it, and I'd witnessed his rapid deterioration. In visualizing my character, Joseph Axel, I suddenly realized how much he resembled a late great-uncle of mine who'd owned a pharmacy in Brooklyn. I knew that memories of visits to that pharmacy would provide scenic material for Joe's flashbacks of better times. So now I had the disease and the profession, but I still needed to know more about each of them. Not too much, though; a novel isn't a medical treatise or a job description. I looked up Parkinson's in my children's encyclopedia and discovered that one of the earliest symptoms is an involuntary hand movement called the "pharmacist's roll"! A lucky coincidence, perhaps, or unconscious knowledge—I'm still not sure. To integrate the facts into the story, I had Joe Axel look up his disease in his grandson's encyclopedia and register the coincidence himself, with bitter amusement. By then I felt I knew him well enough to advance his story.

Yet no matter how much we think we know about these people we've invented, they may surprise us by acting out of character, by doing or saying the unexpected. They don't have to be predictable to be believable. In his discussion (in *Aspects of the Novel*) of "round" and "flat" characters, E. M. Forster says, "The test of a round character is whether it is capable of surprising in a convincing way. If it never surprises it is flat. If it does not convince, it is flat pretending to be round. If [the truly round figure] has the incalculability of life about it—life within the pages of a book."

Once again, showing, not telling, is the best way to achieve that satisfying roundness, to persuade the reader of what Henry James called "felt life." If you sense that you're being manipulated by the manuscript you're reading, it may be because you're being *told* how to feel about the characters, or how they feel, rather than being allowed to figure things out for yourself. Writing "John was mean," is authorial intrusion. Demonstrating how John threatened his little sister, kicked his cat, or bullied his wife lets the reader come to her own conclusion about John's character and temperament. "John was sad" is equally intrusive, and flat. If we see John unable to eat his dinner, to swallow past the lump of grief in his throat, if we see him lying in a darkened room, thinking about his late wife, we *know* he's sad, and we can identify with his sadness. How John reveals his feelings harks back to how well we know him, to those questions the writer asks himself about a character's psyche. For example, if John's wife died, how would he react? We may also simply *infer* John's mood from the events of the story and our previous knowledge of him. Poor old John, who was always such a sensitive boy (remember the way he cried at the movies?) and whose mother died in childbirth, et cetera. When reading workshop manuscripts, it's important to recognize and remark on passages that seem manipulative or inappropriately instructive. The characters must appear to live their lives independent of the writer's control over them. During a focus session on character development, members of the group might read aloud passages from other writers' published works that demonstrate the ways that people are made to come alive on the page.

Completing the writing of a novel is not always a time of unmitigated joy. To turn the book in is to turn the characters in as well, to move out of their neighborhood or evict them from yours. The wrench of parting mutes the satisfaction of having finished the task. It's time, then, to rummage in the imagination for new people, and for fresh language with which to tell their stories. There is for many writers, including me, a terrifying and solitary period after the end of each book, when it seems that all experience, knowledge, emotion, and energy have been expended on that last departed group. This is a far worse time, I think, than one of ordinary social loneliness. So, if you're lying in bed late at night, reading or dreaming, and a madwoman comes knocking at your door, let her in.

14

Where Am I?

Knowing exactly where he is is as important to a writer as it is to a blind man.

—Ross Macdonald

It's not unusual for someone in a workshop to ask, after considering a story, where it takes place. "I'm lost," the reader might say, and if it isn't the writer's intention to be mysterious or disorienting, then something is missing or wrong.

The rendering of place is similar to the rendering of character, in that it's best to show, not tell. Skyscrapers indicate a big city, but unless you conduct a guided tour, pointing out the Sears building or the Trans America Building or the World Trade Center, we may not be sure which big city we're in. Of course there's more to any setting than a mere painted backdrop of buildings or mountains or lakes, like the ones photographers pose their subjects before. What about clotheslines and alleyways, awnings and posters, keyholes and the secret view behind them? Still, both the writer and the workshop reader might ponder why a story takes place here, rather than there; how the landscape affects the plot and the people; and what the true elements of place are, anyway. When Snow White wakes up and murmurs, "Where am I?" does she want to know the exact location of the forest she's in, or will she be satisfied by Prince Charming's time-honored, macho reply, "You're with me"?

When she was ninety, Georgia O'Keeffe wrote, "Where I was born and where and how I have lived is unimportant. It is what I have done with where I have been that should be of interest." On one level, she's directing attention away from herself toward her painting; on another, she's implying that every geographical region offers up its own artistic possibilities. Yet just as I've envied writers who have led more interesting lives than my own, I've often wished I lived in a more exotic setting, like Susannah Moore, whose novels are set in Hawaii, where she spent her childhood, or Isak Dinesen, who could write about Africa with such ease and authority. The geography of fiction, the "sense of place" that critics often refer to in determining the verisimilitude of a piece of fiction, is an essential part of our own conception of a story. I think of "Last night I dreamt I went to Manderley again," and instantly I'm transported. Brooklyn, where I grew up, doesn't have quite the same resonance or panache. But which Brooklyn am I referring to? The built-up borough with its distinct neighborhoods, populated by various ethnic groups, or the farmland the Dutch settlers once tilled, or the forests the native Americans first inhabited and knew? It depends on when the story takes place. So your group discussions about setting in fiction should include a consideration not only of place but also of time.

The indigenous flora and fauna, the architecture, and the language of a place can change radically from generation to generation. In 1930 Dutch elm disease devastated a flourishing species in the American Northeast. Cows don't graze in Brooklyn anymore, and Ebbets Field, where the original Dodgers used to play baseball, is now the site of a huge housing complex. It's hard to believe that once upon a time New York City subway ads were not bilingual or that before the twentieth century, there wasn't any underground system at all. But there are certain constants. If you can see a saguaro cactus from your window, you're in the American Southwest, and if the view is of a tundra, you're in Arctic territory.

Landscape can strongly influence the mood of a story. Think of the long, dark, brooding winters in Sweden or Alaska, and then the sunny relief of the summer solstice. When Chekhov's three sisters long to be in Moscow, they also want to escape the dismal winter landscape of the country. Even a vagueness of place can be telling—about the rootlessness of characters, their sense of not belonging anywhere. My own life, spent largely in Northeastern urban areas like Brooklyn and Manhattan and in the suburbs of Long Island, seemed to dictate limits on where my fictional characters might live. I didn't think that I could "fake" Hawaii or Africa, no matter how many books I'd read about those places, and there were already thousands of stories and novels written about metropolitan and suburban New York. I didn't quite believe the old movie adage: "There are eight million stories in the naked city," or that all of them would be that interesting, anyway. How can the familiar be interesting? I'm reminded of a trip we took to Italy when our children were young. One of them kept speaking in a peculiar accent, and when we asked her why she was doing it, she explained that she wanted people to think she was a foreigner. "You *are* a foreigner here," we told her, but she just didn't get it. And maybe I didn't get it at first, either, when the poet William Stafford said that "all events and experience are local somewhere."

But traveling gave me a broader perspective, and I began to take courage from Henry James's observation that a brief impression, "the merest grain, the speck of truth, of beauty, of reality, scarce visible to the human eye," can be the nucleus for a work of fiction. I also began to see that with a large enough gift for invention you can be an armchair traveler. Anne Tyler said in an interview, "I hate to travel, but writing a novel is like taking a long trip. This way I can stay peacefully at home." What a notion—writing *instead* of experience! In Tyler's novel *The Accidental Tourist*, Macon Leary feels the same way as his creator. He writes guidebooks for a living, cribbing some of the material from other guidebooks, proving that you don't have to be there to tell how it is. This idea is beautifully reinforced by the opening line of Harry Crews's memoir, *A Childhood* (aptly subtitled *The Biography of a Place*): "My first memory is of a time ten years before I was born, and the memory takes place where I have never been and involves my Daddy whom I never knew."

Dante wrote about Hell in grotesque detail, and several hundred years later, so did Stanley Elkin, who referred to its "stinking sulfurous streets," its "pointless, profitless muggings," and "joyless rape," making it sound suspiciously like a terrified tourist's take on New York City. And he sums up Heaven, in typical Elkin fashion, as "rather like a theme park." My own characters, including the ones who've died, didn't enter the Afterlife (not on the page, at least), but some of those among the living began to move as far afield as Seattle or Los Angeles. I even wrote a novel (*Hearts*) in which the protagonists take a trip by car across the continental United States. When someone in my workshop commented, about a certain chapter, that it read like a travelogue, I resisted the criticism at first. I mean, my characters were *traveling*—what did he expect? Then I began to see that although the style was descriptive, inviting attention to everything passed by and through, I'd end up with a volume for every fold of the road map if I didn't hold back. Sometimes whole states had to be rendered in a sentence or two. New Jersey is noted for the industrial darkness of its larger cities, and the approach to California is signaled by the appearance of license plates reading "NICE GUY," "LOVER," "CLASSY," and "CINDY B." New Jersey, the Garden State, really can't be summed up by its industrial darkness any more than vanity plates can capture a state as vast and varied as California. But in a novel, with its intimate account of a handful of people, one has to be selective.

And it's necessary to see the view through the eyes of the characters (another important point to be made in your focus sessions on place). In a reversal of the chameleon's trick, the landscape changes as soon as a particular personality enters it. A depressed person isn't going to take note of the merry tweeting of birds, not without irony, anyway, or a desire to strangle them in their nest. He's more likely to perceive the one dead tree in a verdant arbor, while a rapturously happy character will romanticize even the bleakest scene. The fancy penthouses of Central Park West in Manhattan are only a few doors away from a string of welfare hotels, so the rich and the poor may grow up in the same neighborhood with radically different memories of how things were. And memory can be influenced, too, by the richness or poverty of imagination and desire. Sometimes we see only what we choose to see. Any guidebook to New York City can tell you that Broadway is brilliantly lit; that's why it was dubbed the Great White Way. But the despairing hero of Ralph Ellison's *Invisible Man* can make you believe it is one of the darkest spots in the universe. And the hedonistic teenage girl in *Hearts* marks her journey by the amusement parks and souvenir shops she visits, whereas her stepmother, who's relentlessly self-improving, forces herself to admire the country's natural treasures, even when she's exhausted and dispirited.

It's the writer's challenge to make the surface of Mars familiar and real and the streets of New York new. Certain facts available to anyone lend authority: landmarks, street names, means of transportation. The German writer Karl May used such received information, along with an active imagination, to write a series of immensely popular books about the American West, without ever having been there. It's not difficult to ascertain usable geographical data. If a story takes place in Montana in winter, there's a very good chance of snow, and if it's Arizona in August, it will be hot and dry. But fiction also has its own interior weather that's measurable only by the barometer of the heart.

When my parents were in their eighties, I decided to tape some brief moments of their oral history. I wanted their voices recorded for myself and for the generations to follow, and I wanted to have a stronger sense of how they saw their own lives. Toward the end of the tape, I asked them to speak about the landscape of their respective childhoods—my father's in a remote Bessarabian town called Lipkan, my mother's in bustling, turn-of-the-century Brooklyn, New York. What I was looking for was the exterior visual scene: trees, architecture, the shape of the skyline. I also hoped for an insider's view of the rooms they grew up in. But each of them kept veering off into other areas, mostly related to people: family, neighbors, friends, enemies. My maternal grandparents had a small grocery store and, like the storekeeper in Bernard Malamud's memorable novel *The Assistant*, they frequently extended credit to other poor families. My mother dwelled on the cheapskates who moved without paying the grocer and on how her sickly father had to climb several flights of tenement stairs in a fruitless effort to collect their debts. I tried to switch the focus by asking direct questions about the furniture in her family's apartment and what she could see from the kitchen window. My mother wouldn't be swayed from her side of the story, which was about people, people, people. My father wasn't much more cooperative. He recounted an anecdote I'd heard a hundred times before, about a famous doctor making a house call to Mr. Bloom, an ailing neighbor. "When Bloom asked the doctor if he could eat a little pickled herring, the doctor said, 'Of course! Eat anything you like. You'll be dead in a week, anyway.' "

"Yes, yes," I said impatiently, over his laughter at his own recollection, "but what did your house look like? What kind of roof did it have? And how big were the rooms?" Then my father began to describe his bedroom, the very bed he shared with two of his brothers. *Now* I was getting somewhere. But then he wandered off into that old story about waking in the middle of the night next to his brother George, who seemed to be burning up with a fever. When my father ran to his parents' room to tell them about George, they discovered that *he* was the one with the fever.

After a while I gave up and just let them have their say,

without interference. At the very end of the tape, my mother, her voice made thin and hesitant by the stroke she'd suffered a few years before, says, "When I was a child we had wedding and bar mitzvah parties at home. I remember my cousin Louie's party, in the Bronx. We had to take the El train to get there. I was the oldest, you know, and I was allowed to stay up for the whole thing, while the younger children slept on the pile of coats on the bed. There was dancing. Oh, how I loved to dance! And all the way home the music was still playing in the wheels of the train."

That passage from my mother's memory makes me very happy and sad at once, but what in the world does it, or anything else my parents said, have to do with landscape? Plenty, actually. While I was trying to manipulate their version of their childhood scene, with intrusive questions about foliage and decor, they were telling me vital facts about their *own* view of things. My father's brothers were prominent in his crowded landscape, lying skin to skin with him that way, in a single bed, so that they seemed to have a shared metabolism. They were *part* of the landscape. And what about the tenement stairs my grandfather climbed, and the bed in my mother's story that couldn't really be described because it was covered with coats and sleeping children? And then there was the elevated train to the wilds of the Bronx, speeding over treetops and past other people's lighted apartments, with wedding music playing in its wheels. Not all the details are there in my mother's and father's narratives, but there are a few solid images and many evocative clues. It's up to the listener/reader to fill them in.

If imagined or remembered music can call forth landscape, then other sounds can, too. Grace Paley's story "The Loudest Voice" opens with a veritable orchestra of sound and an instant sense of location.

Where Am I?

*There is a certain place where dumb-waiters boom, doors
slam, dishes crash; every window is a mother's mouth bid-
ding the street shut up, go skate somewhere else, come
home. My voice is the loudest.*

There are more discreet auditory clues. The novelist Hortense Calisher, whose grandmother's furniture had been passed
down to her, once jangled a brass drawer pull on an heirloom
dresser and said, "That's the sound of my childhood." Her memoir, *Age*, beautifully recalls the early life that little jangle evoked
for her. I tried to remember a comparable sound from my own
childhood, and came up with a cacophony of noise that was
more like the background of Paley's story: voices, primarily—we
were a big, talky family living in a small space. Then there was
the city street noise, and radio music, particularly the gorgeous,
static-ridden melancholy of Sunday afternoon opera, sounds
that drowned out my parents' escalating quarrels. Years and
years later, I would write about a troubled young couple leaving
their tiny, crowded city apartment on Sundays to go house
hunting in the suburbs, as a way of curing the husband's peri-
odic depression and restoring their marital happiness. To my
surprise, I didn't see the connection until I was writing this
down. Although we can imagine other places, with varying success, we all can lay claim to a real and fertile landscape of our
own. Pinckney Benedict writes:

*All of my work comes out of Mississippi, out of the dirt
roads and the fields I drive my truck by. The people who
live in this land are the people I've known best throughout
my life, and together with the country we live in, they form
a vast well that will never run dry.*

The reader who feels "lost" when he's trying to follow a workshop manuscript doesn't mean to suggest you have to *name* Mississippi in your story; indeed, that might not even work if the dirt roads and the fields and, especially, the people, aren't manifest to him and, of course, to you.

15

He Said, She Said

"Are you sleeping with Janet?"
"Why? Are you sleeping with Frank?"
"Of course not."
"In that case, I'm not sleeping with Janet."

—JOHN UPDIKE, COUPLES

There have been excellent novels and stories written without any conventional dialogue—by Nabokov and Proust, for instance—but if I were in the proverbial dilemma of having to choose a single book for company on a desert island, I'd opt for one filled with the clatter of conversation. That would be the closest thing to human companionship, for which I'm sure I'd quickly yearn. Talking to one another reminds us that we're still alive and not alone. The child who wakes a sleeping sibling in the dark of their bedroom by asking, "Are you asleep?" is, in effect, asking, "Are you still here? Am I?"

In *Alice in Wonderland*, Alice complains: "What is the use of a book without pictures or conversations?" I confess that the first time I read certain densely written novels, like *Jane Eyre* and *Wuthering Heights*, I felt a little like Alice, and I often skipped impatiently through pages of descriptive prose to get to the heart of the matter, those beautifully wide-bordered pages whose printed text was laid out with the economy and symmetry of poetry: the talking part, the best part.

> *"In the name of all the elves in Christiandom, is that Jane Eyre?" he demanded. "What have you done with me, witch, sorceress? Who is in the room beside you? Have you plotted to drown me?"*
>
> *"I will fetch you a candle, sir; and in heaven's name get up. Somebody has plotted something. You cannot too soon find out who and what it is."*

Well, neither could I, God knows. But going back over *Jane Eyre* as an adult reader, I found beauty and excitement in the dense narrative I had only skimmed as a kid, as well as in the dialogue. It was then that I recognized the fortunate, art-making marriage between harmony and melody, form and color, straight narrative and dialogue.

Just as we can recognize many writers by their narrative style, we come to know them, too, by the way their characters speak. Hemingway's people sound—well, *Hemingwayesque*, outdoorsy and terse. It would be hard to imagine his Nick Adams, for example, standing in for Jane Austen's Mr. Darcy, and not only because of the gaps of gender, geography, and generation between their authors. I mean, Nick would probably track mud, or worse, all over Mrs. Bennet's carpets, and you only have to compare the characters' means of social discourse to get my drift. In *Pride and Prejudice*, Darcy's friend Mr. Bingley urges him to join the festivities at a ball.

> "Come, Darcy," said he, "I must have you dance. I hate to
> see you standing about by yourself in this stupid manner.
> You had much better dance."
>
> "I certainly shall not. You know how I detest it, unless
> I am particularly acquainted with my partner. At such an
> assembly as this, it would be unsupportable. Your sisters
> are engaged, and there is not another woman in the room,
> whom it would not be a punishment to me to stand up
> with."

Now, here are Nick Adams and *his* friend Bill in another kind of social situation:

> "Let's get drunk," Bill said.
> "All right," Nick agreed.

The first conversation, by the way, is overheard by Elizabeth Bennet. Austen wrote no dialogue between men without a woman present because she didn't *know* what men said to one another when they were alone.

In a workshop I attended, the leader had us all test the speaking voices of our fictional characters by taking a long section of pure dialogue and crossing out all the "he saids" and "she saids." We then read these passages aloud to the group to see if everyone could tell who was talking, simply by what they said and the way they said it. I strongly recommend this exercise for your group, and the subject of identifiable dialogue for discussion. We were surprised by how hard it often was to distinguish our characters just by their unadorned speech. But there shouldn't be too much confusion. We may all share a common language, but its variables are infinite, and most of us develop individual rhythms of speech and a propensity for particular words or expressions. I think of Uriah Heep's hypocritical use of "umble" and Mrs. Malaprop's fractured phrases. One might argue that they are caricatures rather than characters, but actual people fall into certain patterns of speaking, too. My mother, for instance, began almost every account with, "The thing of it is, dear. . . ." She called everyone "dear": her own children, salespeople, telephone operators, the doctor, policemen. And she, too, was capable of impressive malapropisms. Encouraging a young man to marry, she told him, "A girl in hand is better than two in a bush," and she once remarked, about a jilting, "She dropped him like a baked potato." My father, who came to America from Bessarabia when he was sixteen, prided himself on the English he'd acquired in night school, despite his peculiar pronunciation of certain words. "I bitch you ladies goodnight," he'd say, to our undying delight and embarrassment. An elderly aunt referred to the dummies in a department store window as the "dopes," and an uncle remarked belligerently, about any feat, from a triple play to a triple bypass, "You think that's easy?" Their distinctive ways of speaking helped to identify these members of my family as much as the color of their hair or the shape of their heads.

When you're developing fictional characters, it's important to reveal their idiosyncrasies without letting their verbal (or physical) tics completely define them. My tough uncle, for instance, attended and cried at all of his nieces' school plays, and my father—despite his original and startling pronunciation of certain words—was an eloquent and popular after-dinner speaker. Like everyone, and as our characters should be, they were complex and often unpredictable beings.

Don't be afraid of writing "he said" or "she said" after the appropriate dialogue, but don't feel obligated to do so after every utterance. I would avoid having anybody chuckle, chortle, or giggle *while* they speak, as in " 'I've never been so happy in my life,' she chuckled. 'Oh, neither have I,' he chortled in reply." Just try it sometime yourself. It's even harder than throwing your voice while drinking a glass of water. Characters *can* ask, demand, stutter, blurt, exclaim, agree, shout, mumble, and mutter certain lines of dialogue—but preferably in moderation.

Although there is such a thing as regional diction, it's not necessarily pandemic. Not everyone in Maine is taciturn, not all southerners sound warmly hospitable, and no one *I* knew in Brooklyn actually ever said "dese" or "dose." I'll bet Walt Whitman didn't, either. Some Alabamans or South Carolinians might drop the "g" in their gerunds or say "chimbley" for chimney and "chirrun" for children; others may not. Reading phonetic dialect can get on people's nerves after a while, anyway. There are subtler but no less significant differences in word choices, grammar, syntax, and even punctuation. "Hey" instead of "Hello," "Y'all come back, now" in place of "Good-bye." One character will ask, "How are you getting along?" while another will say, "How you doing?" A breathless sort will rattle off run-on sentences without the pauses provided by commas. Someone who's unsure of himself will end his declaratory sentences with question marks, as if he's always waiting for validation. And then there's the robotic voice that seems to place a period after every word. You'll notice that in Genesis, when God says, "Let there be light," the phrase is followed by a semicolon, allowing the reader to stop and reflect on the momentousness of the occasion before going on to read, "And there was light." As my uncle would say, "You think that's easy?"

Something else to bear in mind when writing dialogue (and when you're discussing the subject in a focus session) is that we all generally speak differently to different people. Listen to the obsequious manner with which someone addresses his boss, as opposed to the more forthright and casual way he talks to his best friend. Imagine the response of a man to his wife when she informs him that he's speeding. Then think of how he'd answer a state trooper who pulls him over to tell him the same thing. My kids used to make fun of what they called my "telephone voice," which was much more formal and self-conscious than the one I used in speaking to them. And they could often guess whom I was talking to by a particular inflection I'd assume. The way most people answer the phone—from an expectant and cheery "Hello!" to a guarded, suspicious "Yes?"—quickly tells us something about them, and the tone of their conversation reveals their attitude toward the person on the other end of the line.

Dialogue should be used only sparingly for exposition. Characters shouldn't go on for pages to explain things to one another, and thereby to the reader. A wife would never say to her husband,

"Honey, do you remember our honeymoon in the second week of June 1950? We went to Niagara Falls, on the border between Canada and New York, and stayed in that cute little cottage with the toilet that ran all night. For some

> *reason, maybe because we were newly in love, it struck us*
> *as being funny."*

If this information is crucial to the story, it might come out this
way, instead:

> *As their fiftieth wedding anniversary approached, Mary*
> *thought more and more about the past, and she tried to*
> *draw John back again, too, to a time when things like the*
> *broken toilet on their honeymoon seemed hilarious.*
> *"Honey," she said. "Do you ever think of Niagara Falls?"*

Husbands and wives tend to talk to one another in shorthand,
anyway, having been trained by habit to anticipate each other's
remarks. A conversation of a long-married couple might go like
this:

> *"You want to watch—?"*
> *"What's on?"*
> *"I don't know. Where's the—"*
> *"Look on the top of the—"*
> *"Who put it there?"*

In reality, we're all always interrupting one another or trailing
off in the middle of sentences. Ford Maddox Ford wrote, in a re-
membrance of Joseph Conrad:

> *One unalterable rule that we had for the rendering of*
> *conversations—for genuine conversations that are an*
> *exchange of thought, not interrogatories or statements*

of fact—was that no speech of one character could ever
answer the speech that goes before it. This is almost
invariably the case in real life where few people listen,
because they are always preparing their own next
speeches. . . .

Most of us also use a few clichés, frequently repeat ourselves, and manage somehow to communicate in nonsequiturs.

Just a single spoken sentence—"Hello, sailor" or "Scalpel, nurse" or, for that matter, "Let there be light"—can tell you in a flash what someone does for a living. Ditto for the man on the Manhattan street who yells, "Designer watches, ladies, only ten dollars!" and the one who says, "This is a stickup." But our silences can be meaningful, too; there are times when we're simply unable or unwilling to speak. The writer who has fully determined his character's psychology will know intuitively when to remove the quotation marks and venture inside his head. Interior monologue, without the ping-pong effect of dialogue, serves some of the same purposes, by moving the story forward, at least on an emotional level, and revealing some intimate details about the characters. The problems of writing interior monologue are similar to those of writing dialogue. We must ask ourselves if these are the character's true thoughts or if the author is brainwashing him with her own philosophy and grandiloquence. Still, there's usually more room in interior monologue for "writerly" writing, more opportunity to use simile and metaphor less self-consciously than in speech. I don't think I could write fiction if I didn't believe that everyone has a complex and clandestine internal life.

Jayne Anne Phillips says, "There's nothing more moving than hearing somebody talk. To hear a beautician talk about what happens during the day is more interesting to me than a well-crafted short story." Phillips is referring to Studs Terkel's wonderful oral histories, which I would recommend to any fiction writer having trouble with dialogue. Hearing people talk about their days within a well-crafted short story is, to my mind, even more satisfying. But you should be able to tell the people apart without a scorecard. Tess Gallagher writes, "It is one of the hazards of fiction that characters begin to blur together if one doesn't keep their differences strongly in mind." A rather common and serious error among new writers is to have all their characters *sound* the same (and more or less like their creators). You might have to listen closely for individual speech patterns and nuances—they're not all as overt as my mother's malapropisms—but they are there and they're crucial. There's regional dialect, the dialect of age and of youth, and of the educated and the uneducated. Most important, though, is the *personal* dialect, a medley of all of the above, plus that mystical and critical element of *self*, shaded by shyness, nervousness, giddiness, rage, or lust.

Someone for whom English is a second language might sound somewhat formal, using fewer contractions, yet make mistakes a native-born American would not. I think of Nabokov's Russian émigré, Pnin, who continually refers to his American hostess, Joan, as "John." I think of the day I found my elderly father trying, in his thick Yiddish accent, to teach his Haitian-born, French-speaking home attendant to speak English. She was repeating, painstakingly, after him, "I go to voik oily." This single spoken sentence revealed a lot about my father: his good-will in helping a fellow immigrant, a certain innocence, of course, and a certain wiliness, too: the woman he was instructing was notoriously late to "voik." And even when my mother developed aphasia as the result of repeated strokes, her personality was still inherent in her halting, fractured speech. Among the last few phrases she ever spoke were "Hello, dear," and "Drive carefully." I was amazed at how easy it was to translate her more cryptic remarks, because they still reflected the intact character of the woman behind the short-circuited brain. Speaking was such an essential part of our relationship; in her last years, we seemed as attached by the telephone line as we once were by the umbilical cord.

Dialogue was equally important to the mother and stepdaughter in my novel *Hearts*, because they were so emotionally *un*connected. It seemed to me when I began writing about them that they would eventually *talk* their way toward a truce, or even affection, because it's the way most people bond. To my surprise, I discovered the two women in a battle of silence somewhere near the middle of the book. Each of them enters her own nonverbal chamber only to discover herself trapped in an absolute din of thoughts. Robin, who's thirteen, aspires toward a *Guinness Book of World Records* kind of silence. She wonders, with typical hyperbole, "If you didn't use your voice for ten or twenty years, could you lose it?" For her part, Linda suddenly thinks of an article she once read about a couple who have stayed married for fifty years without speaking. She remembers how it had all started with an argument on their honeymoon about the wrong eggs ordered for breakfast. What's happening, of course, is a kind of conversation taking place inside Robin's and Linda's heads, as each considers the possible consequences of not talking. They simply can't disengage. But while Robin muses over losing the ability to speak after "ten or twenty years," Linda wonders if that capacity has already been forfeited because of their brief, stubborn, silent quarrel. Linda is the one to give in first, and when she does, she's elated by the sound of her own voice. "It was thrilling to speak again," she thinks, "like opening one's body willingly to love." So interior monologue has moved the story forward, in a way, and we've found out some private things about the characters, things they were unwilling or unable to tell one another.

Nothing is more revealing of a character's personality or motives than his spoken words and his secret thoughts. Listening to dialogue (and interior monologue) read aloud in your workshop should resemble the guilty pleasure of eavesdropping. And you have the advantage of "joining" the conversation, if only to point out that a particular character just doesn't sound like himself. In focus sessions devoted to dialogue, you might discuss its purposes and pitfalls, taking note, at the same time, of the varying speech patterns within your own group.

16

What's So Funny?

When I lose my power to laugh my heart will break.

—ABRAHAM LINCOLN

Our steaks charbroiled to your likeness.

—AIRPORT RESTAURANT MENU

Recently, a young friend had her first child, via the Lamaze method. The mother was fully alert and watching through an overhead mirror as the baby's head emerged. Just the head, that's all. My friend said that the infant immediately opened its eyes, appeared to look around, and then began screaming. The birth of a genius, I thought, with an immediate fix on the crazy, difficult world. Yet the baby didn't retreat from life; it ultimately shouldered its way through, still screaming, of course. The thing is, I've never heard of a baby who was born laughing (and a smile may just be gas). Laughter usually comes a few months later, provoked by some grown-up face making or the dubious thrill of being tossed in the air by a giant relative. The latter kind of laughter is really a nervous response, the exultation of roller-coaster riders, of danger survived. The laughter that responds to Mommy and Daddy wriggling their noses and ears as they hover like helium balloons over the ráils of the crib is something else—the joy of an absurd surprise.

Once we've learned to laugh, there's no stopping us, even if we have to foster it ourselves with dumb jokes. There were these two Irishmen, Scotsmen, Martians, prostitutes, lightbulbs. Another person's laughter alone is often enough to set us off. I know some people so eager to laugh, for the relief it affords, that they start guffawing before you finish telling a joke, before the pratfall or the pie in the face. Laughter *feels* good; there are even weighty claims made for its therapeutic value. A sort of cheap therapy can be found in the familiar shtick of stand-up comics ("Take my wife—please!"), in lighthearted novels and movies, and in the mindless fun of television sitcoms. In all of these instances, I'm referring to the easy laugh that comes from ridiculing somebody else in a kindly or sadistic way that lets you feel superior to the poor idiot who's the butt of the joke. But there's another kind of laughter that requires a more developed sense of humor and has a greater resonance. It's the laughter that can quickly dissolve into tears, because its comic source verges on the tragic and because it's closely related to the substance of our real lives. Byron wrote, "And if I laugh at any mortal thing, it's that I may not weep," a precursor of that familiar expression, "I laughed 'til I cried." I believe he was referring to what I call "serious laughter," as paradoxical as that may sound. The writer who tries to stimulate serious laughter must sometimes take the risk of offending a few for the delight of many. It means that nothing in the world is sacred, either above or beneath the possibility of absurdity. There are several subjects that are themselves not intrinsically funny—aging, illness, and war among them—yet writers like Muriel Spark, Stanley Elkin, and Joseph Heller have all discovered their innate potential for dark comedy. Adolescence is another seemingly sacrosanct topic, with its blights of acne and social rejection, its headlong plunge from childhood to maturity with never enough preparation for such a metamorphosis. For many people it's the most painful time of their lives. I suspect it was so for Salinger, who conveys that agony with such precision in *The Catcher in the Rye*, at the same time that he captures the exquisite comedy of the soul in transition. Holden's cynical yet abiding sense of humor may be his true redemption.

The members of my childhood family had a healthy sense of humor, which was just as well, since I grew up during the Great Depression, when things weren't all that funny. Jokes about money didn't make you any richer, but they must have somewhat tempered the pain of not having enough. I remember my father saying that if he ever found a million dollars, he'd return it if it had been lost by someone poor. And my uncle loved to repeat the joke about the man who holds out his hand to a rich woman, saying, "I haven't had a bite in two days," whereupon she bites him. Then there was the one about the homeless man who approaches a dowager and says, pleadingly, "I haven't eaten in two days," to which the dowager sternly replies, "Young man, you must force yourself."

I remember shrieks and hoots of laughter from the kitchen, where the women in the family—my grandmother, mother, and aunts—concocted supper and stories, breaking themselves up in the process. We kids hung around to listen and to watch our weak-bladdered aunt, whose laughter always sent her hobbling down the hallway to the bathroom. She ran like a chicken with its legs tied together (a line I would use about the mother in one of my novels, years and years later).

What was so funny? Childbirth, for one thing, which seemed hard to believe once I had a couple of kids myself. The aunt with the bladder problem recalled the nurse in the maternity ward wheeling in a cart of newborns for their first feeding. My aunt looked them over and, noticing one particularly birth-battered baby, whispered, "God, whose mutt is that?" to which the nurse stage-whispered back, "Yours." My mother immediately followed my aunt with her tale of the crowded labor room, in which seven women screamed for their mothers and cursed their husbands, while an eighth kept a dignified silence until she was being examined by an obstetrical nurse, when she emoted, " 'O death, where is thy sting?' " At that moment her waters erupted right in the nurse's face. My mother claimed that she stopped screaming long enough to have a good laugh.

Her own labor turned serious, though, when my sister reversed herself in the womb at the last moment and became a "breech" baby. The doctor went out to the waiting room to inform my father of the complication and to ask if he wanted them to save his wife or the baby. My father said that he was so distraught, he considered jumping out the window but thought better of it when he remembered they were on the first floor. "Ha, ha!" The kitchen crew couldn't stop laughing; pot covers clanged, tears streamed, and my aunt hurried down the hall again.

Looking back, I wondered how my cousin felt about being perceived as a "mutt" by his mother only hours after he was born. Did my mother actually stop screaming to laugh at that Bible-quoting woman in the labor room? Likewise, did my life-loving father ever think of killing himself, even in such a stressful situation? And what about my poor aunt and her physical affliction—was it really that hilarious? The truth is, humor is often cruel, nabbing us in our weaknesses and our failures. The comedy routines of Don Rickles and Joan Rivers depend on personal insults. The laughter is most comfortable when someone famous, like Elizabeth Taylor or Queen Elizabeth—who enjoys all those compensatory career perks—is the object of the fun. But even my lesser-known cousin (whose face straightened itself out a couple of days after the birth trauma) was a good foil, and he doesn't seem to have suffered a permanent self-image problem. As for the veracity of my mother's and father's anecdotes, I suspect they were amended with the telling and retelling, to make them better. It's what storytellers do: embellish, exaggerate, edit. Fiction writers dealing with autobiographical events don't have to stick with the facts if a little fancy footwork improves the story. This is especially true of humor, which often depends on a big stretch of the truth to work. For instance, my father's waiting-room account might have been even funnier if he'd been in the *basement* of the hospital.

My aunt's bladder problem was nothing more than another sight gag to the children of the family, who were so used to sight gags from the movies. We didn't worry that the actor slipping on a banana peel might break his hip or fracture his skull. It was just funny: fully anticipated, yet surprising, the way the best humor is. And my aunt was laughing—not just at whatever witticism she'd just heard, but at her own predicament—which gave the rest of us permission to laugh, too.

In 1815, Charles Lamb wrote in a letter, "Anything awful makes me laugh. I misbehaved once at a funeral." To most people, death may seem like a laugh a century, and funerals the last stronghold of solemnity, but when the mourners in Wallace

Markfield's novel *To an Early Grave* realize they're at the wrong funeral, the situation quickly becomes hilarious. And in what I think is the funniest episode of the old *Mary Tyler Moore Show*, Mary cracks up at services for the late TV personality Chuckles the Clown, who's just been eulogized with his own credo: "A little song, a little dance, a little seltzer down your pants." She feels mortified by her unseemly behavior, but as soon as the minister encourages her to laugh, because Chuckles would have been pleased, she bursts into tears.

I've never lost it at a funeral myself, but I've come pretty close. Once, it started raining at the graveside, which would usually just add to the dolor of the day. But then umbrellas started springing up. A tiny old woman had a Mouseketeers umbrella, complete with perky felt ears, and somebody opened one over the rabbi's head that said "CHANNEL 13 COVERS THE BEST." Maybe you had to be there, but it took a lot of self-control to keep a straight face.

The commercialization of death in our culture presents all sorts of farcical possibilities to the fiction writer. Death may not be funny, but the way we deal with it certainly can be. In Evelyn Waugh's classic comic novel *The Loved One*, the protagonist visits Whispering Glades, a Hollywood mortuary, to make funeral arrangements for a friend who has hanged himself. The cosmetician asks, with the earnest charm of an airline steward,

> *"Is there any individual trait you would like portrayed? Sometimes, for instance, the Waiting Ones like to see a pipe in the Loved One's mouth. Or anything special in his hands? Is there anything specially characteristic of your Loved One? Many like a musical instrument. One lady made her leavetaking holding a telephone."*

After I read that last, I thought I'd make a note of it for my own children. When she was little, my younger daughter said that she intended to stuff me and keep me in her living room after I died. Now I could be a one-of-a-kind telephone stand, useful as well as decorative.

In the middle of writing a scene for one of my novels, about the scattering of someone's ashes in the woods, I began to wonder what would happen if the container failed to open at the right moment. I'd already learned, in a phone call to a crematorium, that they usually have a kind of tricky, childproof lid. Would my character, the widow in the story, have to hit it with a rock to get it open? She *does* have to, as it turns out, and is horrified, as if she's striking her poor dead husband. In her struggles with the container, she remembers wistfully and irreverently that the *deceased* was so good at opening things: jars of olives or peanuts, sardine cans. . . . The world is often genuinely tragic and genuinely funny at the same time. Horace Walpole wrote, "This world is a comedy to those who think, a tragedy to those that feel." To live a full and satisfying life, one must, of course, do both.

There are those who contend that comic writing isn't as "important" as tragic writing, but I think it's simply an elitist attitude that tries to exclude joy from art. Humor that's based on character and story is both honorable and significant. I'm happy if I can make some readers laugh without sacrificing those opportunities to make them feel, as well. Henry Green said, "Laughter relaxes the characters in a novel. And if you *can* make the reader laugh, he is apt to get careless and go on reading." Most of us will do anything to make the reader keep reading, but trying to write humorously is hard and hazardous. Nothing fails quite so miserably as failed comedy. I think the problem usually stems from the writer's earnest determination to be funny, rather than just seeing the humor in the situation he's created and taking it from there. When George Bernard Shaw said, "My way of joking is to tell the truth. It's the funniest joke in the world," he was probably referring to what's there for anyone's taking in our terrible, ludicrous human condition.

Puns can also be humorous, and writers are notorious for their aptitude for wordplay. Nabokov was an absolute master of the game; one of his stories was rejected by the *New Yorker* with a note from the editor saying, "We don't print acrostics." The choice of words can be especially crucial in humor. If you've ever heard anyone kill a joke by telling it the wrong way, you'll know what I mean. One time, in a workshop, I presented a story in which a man asks a woman to dance and then moves her stiffly around the floor. I wanted to use a simile related to construction site machinery, and I'd settled for: "He moved her slowly around the floor like a work crane"—an awkward phrase—because I couldn't come up with anything better at the time. "Bulldozer" sounded bullying, which the man wasn't, and just plain "crane" evoked a picture of the bird of the same name. A cement mixer goes around slowly, but it rotates rather then revolves, so the image didn't work. A man in our group immediately suggested "forklift" and everyone laughed. That image was comically precise and, as he explained, any word with an *f* and a *k* in it is always sort of funny.

Misunderstandings, so prevalent in French farce, are funny, too, as a character goes out one door while someone else comes in through another. The more they do it, the funnier it is. The straight man, who's often the vehicle for the joke, if not its target, is inadvertently amusing in his innocence and goodwill. Remember Margaret Dumont's enduring dignity in the face of the

Marx Brothers' zany madness? My mother had a similar ingenu-
ous charm and the same perfect timing. Once, when my older
sister and I were teenagers, we gave a party for several of our
friends. Our mother was busy preparing refreshments in the
kitchen when someone in the living room began telling a joke
that opened with "What did the mohel [ritual circumsiser] say to
the baby before the circumcision?" As if on cue, Mother
marched in at that penultimate moment, bearing a loaded tray,
and asked sweetly, "Would anyone care for some chopped
liver?" Of course we couldn't stop laughing. The real punch line
of the joke: "It won't be long now," which we heard much later
in the evening, wasn't half as funny as her unintentional, im-
promptu zinger. What made it even funnier (and more touching)
was her pleasure in hearing *us* laugh—our party was a success!—although she didn't know exactly why we were so con-
vulsed.

Sometimes a writer laughs uproariously at his own comic
turn, and nobody else in the workshop gets it. If you have to
explain a joke to the reader, if you have to explain *anything*,
there's definitely a problem. The writer may have left out an earlier reference that would make the story funny to anyone who
read it, or his sense of humor may be too quirky and special for
any audience larger or more removed than his immediate family. Or he just may be too easily tickled by his own humor, a
worrisome tendency, like the writer who can't help sobbing as
he pens the sadder moments in his manuscript. Humor can be
subjective, especially when it depends on cultural references, or
"in" jokes. You might start off a discussion about humor in your
group by telling a joke and gauging the individual responses to
it. Chances are, not everyone in your workshop will consider the
same things funny. But there are common denominators that

usually guarantee a broader, more appreciative audience. The gestural comedy of silent film stars like Charlie Chaplin, Harold Lloyd, and Buster Keaton is enjoyed all over the world. Written comedy can translate well, too, when it surmounts our differences while it reinforces our sameness. What's so funny? Everything, almost—if you tell it right.

17

Between the Sheets

I don't mind what people do, as long as they don't do it in the street and frighten the horses.

—Mrs. Patrick Campbell

One of the first things a new fiction writer must learn is how to get his characters in and out of rooms with the least amount of fuss. The initial tendency is to chronicle every agonizing step:

> "Good-bye," Charles said, picking up his hat and coat from the brass coat stand in the hallway and heading for the front door.
>
> "Good-bye," Melanie called after him as he crossed the marble threshold and went down the paneled hallway. His footsteps echoed.
>
> "Good-bye, good-bye," he called back as he opened the

heavy oak door, letting in a blast of freezing January air.
And then the door slammed.
   "Well, there goes Charles," Melanie said.

Most readers would want to scream, "Just go already!" If we
know that it's January, and all those descriptions are extraneous to the story, it might be best simply to say, "Charles left."
The cinematic cut from one place to another suffices. Finding
Charles in his Wall Street office or in Zaire in the very next
chapter wouldn't disorient the reader in the least. But how does
the writer get his characters in and out of bed with such grace
and expediency? It seems to me that this is rarely done without embarrassment—the writer's, the reader's, and sometimes
everybody's (including the poor characters'). This is especially
true in a workshop situation, where writing becomes a public
act, something capable of frightening (or offending) one's peers,
if not the horses. After all, Charles and Melanie have been fully
clothed until now. Although we've been privy to their secret
hearts in previously presented chapters, we haven't so much as
glimpsed their underwear.

   Writing about sex for the first time is something like having
sex for the first time. There's that same dichotomy of boldness
and shyness. You want to just relax and enjoy it (as my teenage
boyfriend once urged), but you can't help wondering: Am I going
to be good at this? How aggressive should I be? I can't wait to do
it! I wish it were over! (Erotica, written primarily to arouse the
reader, is another matter, and is probably best done with less
self-consciousness.) Some novelists of the more decorous romance genre simply close the bedroom door at the very last moment, the way Mother and Dad used to do. But what canny child
didn't speculate about and finally know somehow the marvelous

and disgusting things going on in there? Hints were dropped all day long; little pitchers had only to keep their big ears and eyes open. You might have heard it in some insinuating dinner-table conversation, the grown-up double-talk that always kept you on the edge of revelation. And didn't Dad come up behind Mother when she was doing the dishes and pinch her or something, and didn't her shrieks of laughter spill over the steaming water? And then there was the bedroom itself. When you marched in clutching your earache the next morning, the room was rank with sexual perfume, and the damp bedcovers had been storm-tossed into disarray. Mother, so sweetly pensive now, and Dad in such a great mood, for a change. You didn't have to actually *witness* the primal scene to be aware of its mysterious joy and tristesse.

The writer, too, can leave significant clues for the reader to follow. In a friend's novel-in-progress, the virginal heroine approaches the apartment of the man she hopes will become her lover. She's trembling with excitement and apprehension. As she's about to knock on his door, she notices that the peephole has been painted over. This troubles her, but she's not certain why. Beyond that, the peephole isn't mentioned, but the image stays in the reader's mind and becomes a subliminal symbol for the character's virginity, for the enigma of events that aren't yet known. The heroine knocks and the man lets her in. The novelist can now choose to let us in, too, on what follows, or shut the door with its painted-over peephole right in our faces—it doesn't really matter. The character's arousal is implicit, and something's going to happen, on the page or in the reader's imagination.

The main problem with the closed door of the chaste romance novel, though, is that it's usually closed on people we don't know or care about in the first place. Take these passages, read out of context from a book in that genre, that record the protagonist's progress into maturity. Page 31: "I was seventeen." Page 34: "I was now eighteen." Page 35: "The years were passing. I was twenty-one." It's no wonder that when this heroine begins to describe her heated feelings for somebody else's husband many pages later, we really don't care. Without the development of psychologically complex characters, none of their subsequent actions, sexual or otherwise, has the power to move us.

And despite television's message to the contrary, the perceptive writer recognizes that sexuality isn't something reserved for a certain social class or age group. Blondes and teenagers don't necessarily have more fun. According to Freud, sexual awareness starts very early, and according to Masters and Johnson, desire never completely dissipates. Sex is a remarkably renewable pleasure, like the rereading of a good book. Reynolds Price's novel *Kate Vaiden* beautifully depicts the sexual awakening of a twelve-year-old girl, and *The Dangerous Age*, by Annette Williams Jaffe, is a potently passionate novel about late love.

But all characters, no matter how lustful, must live in time. The sexual mores and fears peculiar to their particular era are always relevant to the story. At the turn of the century, our friend Melanie might mourn her lost virginity and then have a postcoital vision of dying in childbirth in her four-poster bed. In 1931, she worries about becoming pregnant before she's married. In 1942, when Charles is in the army and they surreptitiously check into a hotel as Sergeant and Mrs. Smith, *he* worries about having contracted syphilis from that camp-following prostitute and passing it on to Melanie. In 1975, Melanie uses the Pill, tries to assess the anatomical nature of

her orgasms—is she having the wrong *kind*?—and is furious because Charles has slept with her sister and her best friend. Toward the end of the century, they meet at a singles bar and are
both so fearful of contracting AIDS that nothing physical tran-
spires between them. In light of AIDS, all casual sexual encoun-
ters in contemporary fiction (not to mention in life) appear
daredevil. Who hasn't yet uttered the seemingly paradoxical
phrase "safe sex" or considered the ubiquitous condom? An
overheard conversation between two seven-year-old boys was
recounted in the "Metropolitan Diary" in the *New York Times*.
The first boy says, "I found a condom on my patio," and the
other boy says, "What's a patio?" We've become so nonchalant
about the subject of sex that even schoolchildren have the vocabulary to talk about it.

But how explicit should one be when writing about sex in
fiction? How do you decide what the reader actually needs to
know? These are good leading questions for a group discussion
on the subject. And because the conversation can be general
rather than specific, some reticent group members may find it
easier to join in. The British novelist Kingsley Amis said, in his
Paris Review interview: "I shy away from explicit sex mainly because it's socially embarrassing. The comparison I usually draw
is with being told these things by an acquaintance—and after
all, the novelist is only an acquaintance, isn't he, as far as the
reader's concerned?"

I took an informal survey among some novelist friends on
the question of literary candor. One stated that nothing in Hemingway is sexier, to his mind, than what Jake Barnes and Lady
Brett *can't* do. Another commented on her own delicacy in these
matters but admitted, "I did mention the toilet paper roll in my
latest novel, and included two cases of genuine nakedness." A

third writer said that she tends to be too graphic and depends on editorial restraint. During a particularly torrid passage in the first draft of her first novel, a character said, coyly and encouragingly, to her lover, "You're disgusting," and someone in her workshop, suggesting the whole passage was too explicit and should be deleted, scribbled in the margin of that page, "I agree!" Yet discretion in writing about sex isn't always the best choice. There are many graphic sexual scenes in literature that really work, from D. H. Lawrence's *Lady Chatterley's Lover* to Sue Miller's *The Good Mother*. And lyrical writing on the subject doesn't have to get in the way of passion, as novels by Cormac McCarthy, James Salter, Jeannette Winterson, and Robert Olen Butler all demonstrate. Butler says, "All the words in the language for our intimate body parts are either clinical and cold or gross and demeaning. So you find yourself having to write around the physical objects that are most involved in the sexual act."

You can, as Butler does, make this familiar activity thrillingly new with figurative language, but beware of coy euphemisms and out-of-control metaphors. Years ago, in *Vanity Fair*, James Walcott quoted some flagrant examples in an article called "Naughty Bits" and subtitled "Sex scenes you can be glad you didn't write (much less live through)." My own favorite was in a notably mechanical mode:

> *She was dry. Like a car that won't turn over, she would strain and strain and the ignition would not catch. . . . Joe was moving like a jackhammer and she was dead inside. . . . He slipped out. . . . "We've been keeping the gates locked for so long, they just don't open. They have to be oiled, softened."*

It's easier to imagine a lug wrench being born from that union than a child. I don't mean to say you can't be metaphorical when writing about sex, if the references are subtle, fresh, and on the mark. A simple simile can be very evocative, as in Margaret Atwood's *Surfacing* when the heroine's lustful lover pushes at her "as though trying to fold up a lawn chair." And think of Shakespeare's observation of "the beast with two backs," or Jacques Prevert's allusion to female genitalia as "the wound impossible to heal." One of the best examples I know is from a student's story, in which the narrator recalls his first sexual experience in a single sentence: "She touched my penis, quickly, the way my mother used to test a hot iron." There's a sizzle to that line that's both literal *and* metaphorical.

As in all kinds of writing, words are all we have to sow on that virginal field of paper. When she's still an inhibited adolescent, the heroine of *The Good Mother* has a record player just for 45s "with a thick phallus for a spindle." Colette's Cheri "raises his velvety eyes to the sky and opens his arms like a victim. 'Take me,' " he then implores—unnecessarily, I would say. When I was writing a scene of a novel in which a young man comes to a crowded breakfast table with an irrepressible erection, I decided to have him modestly hide it with a box of cereal. But what kind of cereal? Sugar Pops? Raisin Bran? Or something more robust and confident, like Life or Total or Wheaties—that breakfast of champions? It wasn't simply a matter of choosing a brand name to help establish time and place but also of finding the right word for the occasion. Finally, I settled on Cheerios, for what I think are obvious reasons. Some word choices are easier to make than others. If Christian names for genitals are silly at best, and repugnant at worst, what about legitimate references to some of the grayer areas of anatomy?

In a workshop once, where a story's love scene had the word *flanks* in it, someone asked what they are, exactly, and someone else replied, "I don't know, but I think my mother used to make pot roast out of them." Which made me wonder if flanks, loins, and other such body parts might not be more of a butcher's idea of paradise than a lover's. "Groin" seems a little better, although it is slightly clinical and not very romantic (my first association is with hernias, not lovemaking). But at least you can locate it without one of those charts that dissect a steer into prime and choice cuts. A euphemism I particularly dislike is "member": "She eyed his impressive member"; "His male member grew tumescent." It makes me think of an exclusive men's club that allows women in only on frivolous occasions. I don't mind more direct and even coarse words, but I'd use them appropriately and sparingly, to preserve their impact.

Some writers are just too reverently serious about sex, which is a shame, since it offers such wonderful opportunities for comedy. Think of all the jokes you've ever enjoyed that included sexual references—all those wedding night jokes (anachronisms now), those silly, nervous gags about virginity, virility, and variety. They may have just provided a way of laughing in the dark, of alleviating anxieties about sex and its inevitable shadow, death. (Woody Allen has said that the only difference between sex and death is that after death you don't feel nauseated.) When you really think about it, sex *is* pretty absurd, especially if other people are doing it. All that tension and tumult, all that fuss over what the so-called lower animals do without actual foreplay and without discussing the whole thing over a postcoital smoke. A favorite pastime for happy lovers is to congratulate themselves on their invention and aptitude and then smugly imagine the sexual incompetence of their friends.

But it is often that very ineptness, the sweet, clumsy, funny horizontal dance of love that can make sexual passages in fiction live. The crude farting noise of separating bellies, someone accidentally banging his head against the wall, or developing a leg cramp in the middle of the act. Let's say Charles has left his sexually inert wife, Gwendolyn, for the pleasures of his acrobatic, hyperkinetic mistress, Melanie. Charles wears his watch to bed and it catches the hair on the back of Melanie's neck. "Wait a minute, don't move," he says, and who wouldn't appreciate the ironic humor of that? Well, maybe not Melanie and Charles. But Gwendolyn would probably relish it, and people do say amusing things to one another in bed, if only to relieve the stress of concentration on performance. Performance itself varies, from the efficient "zipless fuck" in Erica Jong's *Fear of Flying* to the sexual failure so fashionable (at least in fiction) during the era of the antihero, when characters kept rolling away from one another in disappointment. Love *doesn't* mean never having to say you're sorry.

Sometimes the sex act is superfluous if the sexual tension is palpable in a story. And sometimes passion is unrequited and must still be acknowledged. A relatively obscure British poet named Charlotte Mew, who died in 1928, wrote an affecting narrative poem called "The Farmer's Bride," in which the bride in question fears all men and, especially, the consummation of her own marriage. She runs away but is captured and brought home to her bridegroom, who keeps her there without forcing himself on her. This is the final stanza of the poem, which is told in the farmer-bridegroom's voice:

> *She sleeps up in the attic there*
> *Alone, poor maid. 'Tis but a stair*

> *Betwixt us. Oh! my God! the down*
> *The soft young down of her, the brown,*
> *The brown of her—her eyes, her hair, her hair!*

The farmer's unfulfilled longing for his wife in these lines seems as sensual to me as anything I've ever read about the sex act itself. In this instance, at least, less activity is considerably more.

As it is in life, fictional sex can be playful, passionate, melancholy, tender, or rough. Each manuscript must be considered separately, and on its own terms. Reasonable questions to ask yourself about a sexual scene include: Are the characters enjoying this? Am I? If you're offended, don't be afraid to say so. When a passage embarrasses everyone, it may be too graphic for the normal reserve of particular characters, or just poorly written. Sexual moments can be vividly rendered by Molly Bloom's breathless stream of yeses, or by languid murmurs, or by the cold energy of simple friction. It's all according to who's doing it and who's telling it. There may be some people in your workshop who will feel uneasy discussing sexual activity of any kind, even in a general way. But it's an important part of literature, just as it's a natural function of life. It's the writer's responsibility to convey her character's sexual experience as honestly and imaginatively as any other experience germane to the story. And it's the reader/critic's responsibility to treat erotic material with the same serious attention given everything else in the work. After all, it's felt life we're after. The writer and the reader may be, as Kingsley Amis suggests, mere acquaintances, but they can also be considered a couple of consenting adults.

18

Are You There, God?
It's Me, Emma Bovary

Child! Do not throw this book about;
Refrain from the unholy pleasure
Of cutting all the pictures out!
Preserve it as your chiefest treasure.

—HILAIRE BELLOC, DEDICATION IN
THE BAD CHILD'S BOOK OF BEASTS

When she was little, my younger daughter couldn't understand why our family dentist always asked her how old she was as soon as she sat down in his chair. I admitted that he never asked *me* that question and I saw him twice a year, too. I suppose he could not imagine making any other casual conversation with a child. Writing for children is something like talking to them. If you don't give them a metaphorical pinch on the cheek, or talk baby talk, or look for inanely safe subjects, you're off to a good start. (Perhaps the same thing can be said about writing for adults.) Like Judy Blume, Madeline L'Engle, Nancy Willard, Lore Segal, Susan Shreve, Tor Seidler, and other distinguished company, I've worn two literary hats—alternately writing novels for adults and for children. A couple of questions inevitably arise, and they may lead to a lively discussion on the subject: What's the difference between those kinds of books besides their intended audience? And why do we need a separate literature for children, when Dickens, Twain, Swift, and Lewis Carroll can be read with different levels of understanding by people of all ages and with real satisfaction by almost everyone?

Despite some singular one-size-fits-all books, there's still a need for others that acknowledge the important differences between adults and children themselves. Children are not just short people with less political power. They have less personal history to draw on than most adults, and a smaller accumulation of facts, ideas, and opinions. The perspective in a children's book is often that of a child who is relatively new to the world and its marvels. This shouldn't imply the adult's superiority or invite his disdain. Much of that grown-up accumulation, like the stuff we keep in attics and basements, is useless or used to our disadvantage, spoiling the spontaneity we once enjoyed as children. The children's book writer Natalie Babbitt says, "What, in the very simplest terms, is a child, after all, but an unrepressed adult? What is maturity, that supposed nirvana we seem never fully to achieve, but total emotional control learned from confrontation with that old apocalypt, experience, which teaches us the necessity for compromise?"

Yet the original intention of a special literature aimed, like a guided missile, at young people was to give them the advantage of our wisdom and years. The earliest children's books are sternly moralistic. Before the invention of movable type, they were all written by monastic teachers for the youngest members of wealthy families, proving, I guess, that privilege has its drawbacks. These books were not meant to delight or distract but rather to be pointedly instructive. The first children's book printed in North America, in 1684, was called *Spiritual Milk for Boston Babies*, and its subtitle read, *Drawn Out of the Breasts of Both Testaments for Their Soul's Nourishment.* A far cry from *Goodnight Moon.* But our expectations of children have changed as radically as their reading matter. In the current pleasure-oriented society of childhood, anything offered as being good for you is automatically suspect, whether it's a green vegetable, an inoculation, or a boring book.

Many of us, at some point in our adult lives, decide it would be a cinch to write a children's book. The brainstorm usually hits while we're lying at the foot of a child's bed reading aloud from some drivel that was actually published and then sold to an unsuspecting parent or grandparent (the middleman between the children's book writer and the child). The offending book is often told in whimsical rhyme, is cloying and simplistic, and hasn't a drop of real wit or style. Why, I can do better than that, the reader thinks, probably rightly. *Anybody* can do better than to insult one's audience. To write a worthy children's book, we have to aim a lot higher, as high as we do when we're writing other kinds of fiction. Like all of us, children primarily want a good story; they want to be beguiled and persuaded and transported. Strong characters are as essential to their books as they are to our own. Because recognition is a key factor, many successful children's books have child-heroes. As always, dialogue should suit the speaker, and a child's language skills usually grow along with the rest of him, but the worst mistake you can make in writing for children is to talk down to them, to limit the narrative vocabulary for the sake of easy reading. Several years ago, at a meeting of the American Library Association, a group of librarians read aloud, in chorus, the following parody of a child-size "abridgement" of *Jane Eyre*:

> *This is Jane.*
> *Hello Jane!*
> *Jane is poor.*
> *Her dress is poor.*
> *Her shoes are poor.*
> *Her hat is poor.*
> *Poor Jane.*
> *This is Mr. Rochester.*
> *Hello, Mr. Rochester.*
> *Mr. Rochester is rich.*
> *He has a big house.*
> *He has a big dog.*
> *He has a big secret.*
> *What is Mr. Rochester's secret?*
> *Jane cannot guess the secret.*
> *Can you guess the secret?*
> *This is Mrs. Rochester.*
> *Hello, Mrs. Rochester!*
> *Mrs. Rochester is crazy.*
> *She has a candle.*
> *The candle is lighted.*
> *Mrs. Rochester can laugh.*
> *She laughs. Ha-ha-ha.*
> *Run, Jane, run!*

Their point was hilariously well made; young readers love *Jane Eyre* in its original version, even if, like me, they sometimes skip ahead to the choicest parts. Edward Rochester's flamboyantly romantic first appearance on horseback—that "positive tramp, tramp, a metallic clatter"—has probably helped more horse-obsessed preadolescent girls make the transition to boys than any other work of literature. The language certainly doesn't get in the way. The novels of E. B. White and William Steig are other models of excellent books with extensive vocabularies that generations of children read and thoroughly enjoy. In *Charlotte's Web*, White pulls it off by having Charlotte, a kindly but didactic spider, define the big words she uses when speaking to her friend Wilbur, a less-informed pig, which is very different from a didactic *writer* explaining things to the less-informed reader. On a single page in Steig's *Abel's Island*, I found the words "internally," "vibrating," and "resolute." It doesn't matter if they demand a few trips to the dictionary, when television necessitates frequent runs to the refrigerator and the bathroom, just to break the trance of ennui.

If language doesn't have to be totally restricted, what about theme? Isn't childhood the last frontier of innocence? Among the jingles that have grown out of children's street games over the years, I found the following:

> *Postman, postman, do your duty,*
> *Here comes Susy, the American beauty.*
> *She can wibble,*
> *She can wobble,*
> *She can do the split.*
> *She can wear her dresses,*
> *Way up to her hips.*

and:

> *Mother, mother, I am sick,*
> *Call the doctor, quick, quick, quick!*
> *Doctor, doctor, will I die?*
> *Yes, my darling, by and by.*
> *How many hours will I live?*
> *How many hearses will I have?*

These rhymes demonstrate that children have always known a lot more than we think they do, even about sex and mortality. And if you visit the children's section in the library, you'll discover an abundance of books that deal openly with such controversial subjects as divorce, alcoholism, drug use, suicide, and, of course, sex. The heavy breathing in some adolescent literature isn't just adenoidal, but breakthrough novels like Judy Blume's *Forever*, in which romance, lust, and even the mechanics of sex are frankly discussed, are often banned or kept under nervous guard at the front desk.

When my husband was about twelve years old, and very curious about sexual matters, he began to look up relevant words in the dictionary. Unfortunately, he wasn't a very good speller and he tried in vain to find *whore* under the *h*'s. But then he heard that *Studs Lonigan*, by James T. Farrell, was a "hot" book. He went to the library, after cleverly borrowing his father's adult card, and discovered that *Studs* was not on the shelf for the taking. Undeterred, he asked the librarian if she had any books written by Farrell. She peered at him over her glasses and asked, imperiously, "The literature or the criticism?" Of course he didn't know what she was talking about, and he was convinced, by her stern expression, that she could read his dirty little mind. Blushing, stuttering, he managed to say "The second one," and, of course, his sexual education was put on hold for a while.

Some people believe you have to have children yourself to be able to write for them, but as Maurice Sendak says, you only have to have *been* a child once. Lois Lowry wrote, about reviving memories of her own childhood: "I have only to press the mental key that calls up each year: 1941 (nursery school: I snitched a blue crayon and wrote my name on my cot during naptime. . . .); 1945 (the fourth grade bully named Gene; the stain on my blanket under my cat after she gave birth to kittens in the attic)." Judy Blume claims to remember her entire fourth-grade experience, and her book *Tales of a Fourth Grade Nothing* bears this out. But even those of us who don't have total recall of childhood events can usually summon up, with startling clarity, the way we *felt.* If you endow your characters with the authenticity of their emotions, then it's just a matter of inventing the circumstances of their story. And as far as the story itself goes, anything that falls under the giant heading of human interaction is suitable for a children's book.

Someone in your discussion group might logically ask if the writer has a greater obligation to be truthful when writing on important subjects for such an impressionable audience. E. B. White says, "In a free country, a writer's duty is to have no duties." But in 1881, Robert Louis Stevenson wrote, "There are two duties incumbent upon any man who enters on the business of writing: truth to fact and a good spirit in the treatment." Telling the truth, though, doesn't mean driving it in with a sledgehammer, turning honest fiction into mere tracts. As the old saying goes, if you want to send a message, use Western Union. And truth telling doesn't preclude taking certain liberties with surface reality. Young readers are especially tolerant of fantasy or myth, as long as it contains inherent truths. If a pig or a rabbit in a book wears a hat and coat and takes a bus to work, children don't demand that it be an allegory, nor do they expect a moral at the end, although occasionally they supply one of their own. They only want to be convinced of that particular pig or rabbit as a character. At least for a while. One of my own children must have undergone a literary growth spurt right before she firmly announced, at the library one day, "No more books with talking animals!"

Good novels, for any audience, while not deliberately polemical, often turn out to be instructive. This is what psychologists call incidental learning. If humor is present in the work, the process is more pleasurable. Humor is as vital in fiction as it is in life. It brings instant relief in moments of embarrassment and fear; it's that extra dimension that makes our condition bearable. Children request funny books for the solace and distraction they offer. But they ask for sad ones, too, to help them cope with some unexpressed sorrow of their own. Just as we do.

Are there any major differences, then, between books written for adults and those for children? In *Childhood to Childhood*, Jean Karl writes, "A children's book looks at life with hope, even when it's painting the most disastrous of circumstances. . . . When hope is gone, childhood is gone." I'm sure she didn't mean to imply false saccharine hope about inevitabilities like aging, illness, and death. It isn't the author's responsibility to provide happy endings when even God doesn't do that. In 1905, Joseph Conrad wrote: "To be hopeful in an artistic sense, it is not necessary to think that the world is good. It is enough to believe that there is no impossibility of its being made so." In some cases, it's just a matter of balancing the bad news with some good news, as White does in *Charlotte's Web*. Charlotte sums up life ruefully when she tells Wilbur, "We're born, we live a little, we die," and indeed she *does* die in the short span of the book, but not before she saves Wilbur's life, a life he ebulliently enjoys. In one of my novels written for children, an elderly, ailing dog is put down at the vet's. A twelve-year-old boy in Kansas wrote to tell me that his dog was getting old, too, and the book had made him sad, but that it also made him happier, somehow. What he wrote, exactly, was, "Your book fills me with feelings of sadness, gladness, and well-being." Maybe he felt less alone in his experience, or maybe he'd expended some of his anticipated grief on the fictional dog.

Young readers are indefatigable letter writers, and they're not always motivated by admiration. Sometimes they write because of a class assignment: "Dear Mrs. Wolitzer, This is Author Week at Weehawken Middle School and I got you." The hidden text, of course, is that the writer really wished she'd gotten Judy Blume, instead, and I can't say that I blame her. But sometimes the letter is a spontaneous response to your book, which is, unfortunately, no guarantee of praise or gratitude. The book may have been assigned, too, and kids tend to be disconcertingly candid in their opinions. A fifth-grader once wrote to tell me, "I liked your book. The first page was the best part." Scott O'Dell, a very popular children's writer, received a letter from a child who said several flattering things that appeared to have been prompted by an elder, before signing off with "Well, goodbye for now you old jerk!" And one of Maurice Sendak's young readers dropped him a line just to say, "I hope you die." In Beverly Cleary's delightful epistolary novel *Dear Mr. Henshaw*, a ten-year-old boy adds this postscript to his letter to an author, in reference to one of his books: "I bought a copy of *Ways to Amuse a Dog* at a garage sale. I hope you don't mind."

I've found that novels written for children are perceived by them as the coming attractions of life. If my protagonists are twelve years old, my readers are usually ten or eleven, but I don't write with a particular audience in mind, except, perhaps, for the child I once was. Reinhabiting my twelve-year-old self is a lot easier than getting into last year's bathing suit. Of course, all novels with young heroes are not necessarily children's books. In Henry James's *What Maisie Knew* and Alison Lurie's *Only Children*, it's the corrupt and cryptic adult world the child witnesses, rather than her own. The child reports what she sees and hears, and the adult reader makes an interpretation.

A popular bridge between books for kids and those for grown-ups came about with the establishment of the young adult novel, or the "Y.A.," as it's commonly known. Many of these books address the concerns of the adolescent, who is still clumsily straddling both worlds. When writing for emerging adults, there is a danger of becoming parental and trying to "guide" them toward maturity. The result, too often, is a preachy and patronizing book. People in your workshop (who were once discerning youngsters themselves) will be quick to point this out. In books for any age group, a good story and strong charac- ters are what matter, not moral instruction. That's why *Romeo and Juliet* is so moving, and an updated Y.A. version, in which a high school guidance counselor lectures the young lovers on why it's better to abstain from sex, is not. Whitewashing the world kids are about to inherit is another familiar mistake. Ur- sula Nordstrom, the noted editor of children's books, wrote:

> Is there a real world where young people always *respect*
> their always *respectable parents? Where Dick Faversham*
> always *asks Patty Fairchild to the Senior Prom? Where*

Dan Baxter, the bully, and Mump, his toady, always get
their comeuppance? The "rigid world of good and bad" is
infinitely easier to write about than the real world.
Because the writer of books about the real world has to
dig deep and tell the truth.

Picture books, for the very youngest, often prereading, child, have their own structure. They're almost always thirty-two pages long, and they look like little poems on the manuscript page, although they don't necessarily have to rhyme. Descriptive writing should be kept to a minimum because the visual images are rendered by the illustrator. The most significant thing about picture books is that they're read aloud, over and over again (maybe they ought to be called listen-and-look books). Like poems, they're often committed to memory, by both children and their parents. The text may be brief, but it shouldn't skimp on the richness of its language, meaning, or musicality.

Bearing all of the above in mind, workshop members should address manuscripts written for children very much the way they do the ones written for adults. If you're bored, it's because the writing needs work, not because the story is too "young" for you. It's necessary to ask the same questions you would about any manuscript, regarding willing suspension of disbelief, character and plot development, fictional voice, emotional and narrative suspense, and general readability. To do any less is to disrespect the writer *and* his potential readers.

And whom should the would-be children's book writer be reading? Tolstoy, Joyce, Chekhov, Gertrude Stein, Colette, Faulkner, Muriel Spark, Graham Greene, William Kennedy, and Donald Barthelme, among others. They all wrote books for children (Barthelme's National Book Award was in that category), although sometimes just for one particular beloved child. A visit to the children's room at the public library isn't a bad idea. If you feel conspicuously tall there, as I do, borrow a small child for cover, and to help you find good books on the lowest shelves.

19

Hollywood, Here I Come!

PRODUCER: *"I'm a big fan of yours."*
WRITER: *"Gee, you've read my books?"*
PRODUCER: *"Well, not personally."*

—ANONYMOUS

Most serious writers I know (even those who enjoy movies) publicly disparage Hollywood but privately yearn for its tawdry glamour and those alleged big bucks. They've read the horrific accounts of how screenwriting wasted the gifts and damaged the lives of F. Scott Fitzgerald, William Faulkner, and Nathanael West. But those stories are probably counteracted by the happier experiences of novelists like Diane Johnson (who adapted Stephen King's *The Shining* for the screen), Richard Price, and John Sayles, all of whom seem to have kept their literary powers and their integrity intact. And many writers remember with pleasure their own early fascination with the silver screen and its ongoing, positive influence on their work.

So Hollywood's siren call is usually pervasive enough to warrant a focus session or two on screenwriting. Members of your workshop may want to find out how to break into the business and whether the leap from writing fiction to writing screenplays is a natural one.

I've always loved going to the movies. When I was a child, there was a children's section in the Marlboro Theater, our local movie palace, overseen by a Nurse Ratched–type matron in a white uniform, so I got to go by myself pretty often. There, in the filtered darkness, I glimpsed the previously unknown worlds of politics, commerce, and romance. Romance was the best. I suppose my parents loved one another in their embattled way, but it was nothing like the way Humphrey Bogart and Ingrid Bergman loved one another in *Casablanca.* To my knowledge, my father never said to my mother, "Where I'm going, you can't follow—what I have to do—you can be no part of. . . . Someday you'll understand that. Not now. Here's looking at you, kid."

Of course that was nothing but cinematic make-believe. *Nobody's* parents spoke to one another that way, at least not in our neighborhood. Indeed, having a couple of kids might have ended things between Ilsa and Rick even faster than the war and her inconvenient marriage to Victor Laszlo. But I was pretty young when I saw *Casablanca.* Although World War II was under way off the screen, as well as on, it was only a distant fact to most American children, and I was desperate to make believe, to escape from the dreary reality of ordinary middle-class life—the very stuff I would later return to in my fiction, with such gratitude and satisfaction.

In the meantime, there was the continuing, extravagant sideshow of the movies: Fred Astaire and Ginger Rogers punctuating their dialogue with fits of tap dancing and bursts of song, George Raft and Edward G. Robinson making their final points with bursts of gunfire. I was crazy about the nonsense syllables of Carmen Miranda's "Chicka-chicka-boom-chick!" and Bette Davis's clipped pronouncements, heightened by her exophthalmic gaze. I enjoy them even now, despite their absurdity, maybe *because* of their absurdity. Many fiction writers share this particular nostalgia. Novelist and film critic Jonathan Baumbach says,

> *Movies were our own discovery, an outlaw pleasure. We had no obligation to value them as art, to find ourselves changed by them. Our relationship to movies was nobody's business but our own. It was an illicit affair, so all the more charged with mystery. In some ways, the more banal the film, the deeper the fantasies it generated.*

And toward the end of *The Journals of John Cheever*, when he's extremely ill and weary, Cheever remarks on "the absence of anything that strikes me as truly genuine. . . ." He continues:

> *So I am pleased to make coffee in the kitchen and chat with the old dog. I am Bette Davis and the dog is Geraldine Fitzgerald in the last scene of* Dark Victory. *"Now we can learn to live again," says the old dog, and I say, "If I can laugh, I can live." I then begin to laugh, quite tirelessly, while the crawlcredits—which are, in this case, exhaustive—commence.*

Whenever I came home from those early double features, I'd head straight for the sanctity of the bathroom, where, with a sorry absence of Cheever's irony, I would repeat as much of the movies' dialogue as I could remember into the mirror, improvising what I couldn't remember, kissing my own arm when necessary, dancing around on the tiled floor, and singing into a bar of soap. I'd stay in there until someone else banged on the door to get in. If we weren't a one-bathroom family, I might be a famous actress or director today.

Without my mother there to protect my eyesight, I always chose to sit in the front row of those plush red velvet seats at the Marlboro so I could be as close as possible to the screen. Like Mia Farrow, in *The Purple Rose of Cairo*, I wanted to *enter* each movie and become part of the life it depicted. After I grew up and became a writer, I was offered what seemed like the next best thing—the chance to write for the movies or, more precisely, to *rewrite* one of my novels for the big screen.

Over the years, several of my books have been optioned for the movies, but, alas, I've always remained an option, never a bride. In most cases, someone else was engaged to write the screenplay. At first, this struck me as utterly contrary. Why not hire the original writer, the one who knows the characters and their story by heart, rather than a total stranger? After a few stabs at screenwriting, I began to understand why novelists aren't in the forefront of the movie industry. My first chance to adapt something of my own occurred with my first novel, *Ending*. Bob Fosse had optioned it right after it was published, and Robert Alan Arthur, a talented and experienced screenwriter, was given the job of adapting it. After several drafts and as many renewals of the option, the project was finally dropped (as most of them are). A few years later, I was asked to adapt the book for a television movie. My first attempt was abysmal. As ordered, I wrote a "treatment," which sounds therapeutic but is only the equivalent of a summary or outline. This was something I'd never chosen to do with my fiction because I like to discover what happens as I go along. But it was sort of fun and not very difficult. Then I started to write the teleplay, and that's where I ran into serious trouble. I couldn't manage to exclude any part of the novel, or even change it very much, and since there's so much interior monologue, the dramatic level was pretty low. It's hard to write a movie about someone *thinking* more than she's *doing*. You'd just end up with a character standing there for a couple of hours, with her voice-over thoughts playing on a soundtrack (not exactly the stuff of big box office). But the most profound shock of all was that screenplays aren't really about language, the way much of fiction is. Even though I can remember almost every word that Rick and Ilsa and Rico and Shane said, action and a careful structure are at the core of most successful movies.

Before I tried to adapt my second novel, as a feature film this time, I read a few books about writing for the screen, and a couple of actual screenplays, too. They gave me a crash course in the language of the trade. What I'd always thought of as character development became "character arc," a final draft turned into a "polish," and the "bible" of a TV series might feature the Simpsons rather than the Israelites. I also discovered that screenwriting, unlike fiction writing, has stringent rules about structure and format. Nowadays, there's scriptwriting software that really helps, but back then I had to figure it out for myself. Near the beginning of my novel *In the Flesh*, which is told in the first person, the heroine, Paulie, and her husband are awaiting the birth of their first child. A friend shows them her own delivery-room photographs and offers to lend them her camera. An ensuing passage reads, "We had decided against delivery-room photographs for ourselves. Everything would be recorded perfectly in the darkroom of the heart." I liked that second line and hoped to squeeze it into the screenplay, somehow; maybe Paulie could just *say* it. Let me tell you, it was impossible to turn that bit of introspection into dialogue. Absolutely *no one* ever says, "Everything will be recorded perfectly in the darkroom of the heart." I had to settle for the character gesturing at her chest and saying, "I'll remember it here." Just because something looks good on the page doesn't mean it will play on the screen. And every little scene or turn of plot in a novel doesn't necessarily work dramatically or fit into the prescribed three-act structure for feature films or the seven-act format for television movies. Read a few novels that have been adapted for the screen and then read the screenplays. You might even decide to present comparative excerpts at one of your focus sessions, to demonstrate the process and the problems of adaptation. I think you'll see that your book must be completely reconceived if you plan to tailor it for another medium. And be prepared for other people's reconceptions of it, too; they may not match yours.

The primary advantage of fiction writing (after the inexpensive wardrobe) is the autonomy the writer enjoys. Despite workshop criticism and the ultimate input of editors, the work is solely yours. No one can alter it without your consent, and you can take all the credit (or blame) yourself. This is decidedly not so when you're writing for television or the movies. Only a few people, like Woody Allen or Steven Spielberg, have complete control over the production of their projects. The rest of us must take part in what's called a "collaborative" effort, though it seems like something far less congenial. It's difficult to see how any creative work can ever be truly collaborative, anyway, except when one's duties are carefully determined and separate, as in songwriting or picture books. If individual visions don't clash, then egos will. I remember trying to compose a round-robin story with a bunch of writers at Bread Loaf one evening. It was supposed to be a sort of party game, but writers are always serious, to some extent, about writing. We were each allowed to contribute one word at a time, but no one wanted to waste his or her turn on something as insignificant as "the" or "a" or "and," so the "story" ended up being a compendium of fancy words that didn't make any sense at all.

Two writers I know, Clark Blaise and Bharati Mukherjee, who are married to each other, have actually cowritten a couple of books. When I asked them to tell me precisely how it's done, they reminded me that although they both write novels and short stories, they only conspire on books of nonfiction, for which the workload of research and writing can easily be divided. Clark, for instance, would interview people, and Bharati would transcribe his tapes, and vice versa. Or one would be assigned the historical and religious facts, and the other the more personal human events. "We edit one another. We argue and then compromise," Bharati said. But when I pinned her down, when I asked if she still knew which sentences, which phrases, which individual *words* in the final manuscript were hers alone, she admitted that she did. She would know them anywhere, just as I suspected she would, and just as one can immediately pick out one's own child in a crowd of other people's children. A few moments later Clark admitted to recognizing his words, too, words that had occurred to him, prior to any discussion about the book with Bharati, in the privacy of his own head. Fiction writing is a personal, perilous, but independent act of invention, which eventually evolves into a noninvasive kind of collaboration between the writer and the reader.

Screenwriting is hardly ever that spontaneous and autonomous, except when a script is written "on spec" (without a contract but with the intention of trying to sell it after it's done). Usually, before a single word of an assigned screenplay or teleplay is written, there are edicts from above. Meetings (pitches) are arranged with executives who proffer preemptive notes on the project. For one television movie script that I was assigned to write (based on a true story about group therapy), I was forewarned that there were to be no talking heads and no flashbacks. Be humorous, they said. Be serious. Make everyone sympathetic. Make it credible. Make it snappy. And insert a hook at the end of each act that will keep that trigger-happy crowd from reaching for the remote control. Once the project was under way, I was overwhelmed by the amount of rewriting—not mine, which I was prepared to do—but *theirs*. The first time my script was returned with the actress/producer's new dialogue neatly typed into it, I was shocked. Surely she'd meant to consult me about it first. But that's not the way it works. Robert Louis Stevenson's truism that "in all works of art, widely speaking, it is first of all the author's attitude that is narrated," is obviously not a Hollywood byword. Mine was far from a singular experience. Mordecai Richler says, in his essay "Writing for the Movies":

> *Like most novelists, I am conditioned to working for months on material I discuss with nobody, because to talk about it is to risk losing it. To adjust from that to scriptwriting, where you are bound to meet once a week*

*with a director or producer or both to discuss work in
shaky first-draft form and work yet to be done, is more
than unnerving, it's indecent.*

Fiction writers may depend on their unique vision of
things—colored, perhaps, by workshop or editorial suggestions—but screenwriters always get unsolicited "help," not only
from producers, actors, and directors but also from various as-
sistants of the same. You are simply a hired hand in Hollywood,
even when the original material is your own. No wonder there's
a popular joke out there about the starlet who's so dumb she
sleeps with the writer.

To my surprise, much of the writing imposed on my script
was quite good. It was easy to see that the briefer, brisker dialogue would "play" much better than mine. I was learning a
brand-new skill—writing drama—which I had gone at before
with only blind hope and intuition. And by relinquishing artistic
control, I was loosening up in ways that would probably prove
beneficial in other areas of my life. The whole procedure took
much longer and many more drafts (I mean polishes) than I'd
expected. But finally, after two years, hundreds of phone conferences, and three trips to California, it was done. The script was
accepted, and the money—which was as good as advertised—
was promptly paid. Hollywood isn't so bad, I thought. (I'd forgotten that I'd said the same thing about childbirth during the early
stages of labor.) I decided that the industry is just an easy target for cynics; why, it even makes fun of itself. Movies such as
The Player, The Loved One, The Day of the Locust, and *Barton
Fink* are pretty ruthless in their satire. A couple of years ago, a
"Doonesbury" cartoon that appeared in the (Screen) Writers
Guild of America bulletin poked fun at hiring practices at the

networks. In a phone conversation an agent complains to a producer about his writer client being turned down for a TV series.
"We're producing a young show here," the producer says, "and
we don't hire writers who are old and out of touch." The agent
indignantly replies, "Old and out of touch? Arnie's barely thirty!"
"He wrote on 'Seinfeld,' Sid!" the producer exclaims. "A show
that's been dead for *months!*" The upshot is that Sid, the agent,
who offers a diatribe against Hollywood ageism, is only twenty-
six himself. Ha-ha. Well, they'd hired me, anyway, and Horton
Foote was still working, as far as I knew.

And then the hotly anticipated phone call came from the senior network executive attached to my project. "I have some
good news and some bad news," he began. I thought of all those
good news–bad news jokes about people dying, and I knew instinctively that if this were a joke I wouldn't be laughing at the
punch line. I received the good news first: the network had decided to produce the movie. I understood that this was not a minor accomplishment; only a small number of developed projects
ever actually go into production. But before I could even begin
to feel triumphant, he gave me the bad news. They'd hired another writer to redo the script.

Why am I telling you all this? Not, as you may think, as a
warning against the evils of Hollywood (well, maybe a little bit),
but as preparation for a different kind of writing experience, in
case you, or someone in your group, decide to try it. I'd also like
to celebrate my return to fiction, to writing in solitude but not
loneliness. To think that I could fill up the whole page again, not
just the middle! That characters could have inner thoughts and
unlimited dialogue! That events could be rendered through
metaphor and simile! That every scene didn't have to end in a
cliffhanger or a commercial!

When your story is presented in the workshop, you'll hear plenty of *suggestions* for revision, but no one will lay a hand on it without your consent. Never mind that millions of people still remember who shot J. R. and that when you're introduced to someone as a writer, chances are you'll be asked, politely and doubtfully, "Should I have heard of you?" Never mind that you'll probably wonder (as I do) if every cushion you ever sit on is filled with one of your shredded books. Simply rejoice in your blessed anonymity and autonomy.

20

Working Out

Reading is to the mind what exercise is to the body.

—RICHARD STEELE

've always believed that exercises should be confined to the gym, but a number of people I respect and admire maintain that writing exercises can be really helpful in the fiction work-shop, especially for anyone stalled in her work. Novelist Abigail Thomas leads a group in New York City that functions primarily through writing assignments. She might read a poem aloud and then, picking up on a single line or on the central theme of the poem, or just its title, give the homework assignment of writing a few pages of prose in response. At other times, she'll prompt the group with some seemingly disparate words, like "a horse, a red dress, and a boy named Fred" or "a sandwich, a newspaper, and a pair of new shoes," and ask everyone to write two pages containing those words.

When I asked how this sort of assignment worked, one participant said, "I get ideas for something important from something unimportant." Another woman compared writing these short pieces to playing etudes in preparation for a symphonic concert. The very brevity of the assignments was freeing to those writers who said that they balk and freeze at the notion of beginning a long work. Thomas spoke about the writer who's stuck in the middle of a novel. "Buying a pair of new shoes or a newspaper gives the characters something to do, and who knows what will follow?" I could see the possibilities. The new shoes pinch, making the heroine sit down on a park bench next to a man. They begin a conversation and end up sharing a sandwich. . . . Or, she opens the newspaper and discovers that her ex-husband has married again. . . . Someone else in the workshop said that a set of similar prompts sparked an entire novel for her.

Laura Foreman, citing Rilke's words "In a dark time, the eye begins to see," has her students close their eyes, observe what they see behind their eyelids, and then write about it. For another workshop exercise, she says, "Imagine that you are describing to a police sketch artist what a missing person looks like . . . and that person is *you*. Without looking in a mirror, describe in realistic detail what your face looks like, beginning with the top of your head and ending with the tip of your chin." An auxiliary exercise might have the writer describe herself *without* using a single realistic detail.

Jonathan Baumbach, who directs the writing program at Brooklyn College, suggests that his students write about a re-

cent dream, in order to bring themselves closer to their unconscious. John Gardner used to ask his students to describe a tree
in a manner that tells us as much about the person describing it
as it does about the tree itself. He also suggested that they type
out a masterpiece such as James Joyce's "The Dead." (This can
be a humbling and inspiring experience at once.)

Rosellen Brown advises: "Have a bag of miscellaneous stop-
gap ideas for the days when nothing 'important' will come. . . .
Retell old stories, fairy tales, myths, in new forms. Translate;
translate from a language you don't know. . . . Make a list of all
the things you know: how to make fudge, how to give the Heim-
lich maneuver, how to get from New York to Miami on five dollars. You will have a new respect for all you have mastered and
all you might write out of."

Ron Hansen uses a literary form of Mad Libs, a commercial
party game that my children loved. He'll offer a sentence, with
certain words missing. It would look something like this:

*Last night I saw [proper noun] doing [noun] and it made
me [verb].*

His students fill in the blanks with surprising variety, which
helps them to recognize their individuality of voice and vision,
even when they're kindled by a common prompt.

Writers, especially poets, have long been inspired by paint-
ings and sculpture, which expand their understanding of composition and their ways of looking at things. A. S. Byatt, whose
fiction is filled with impressions of the visual world, has written
several short stories based on the works of Matisse and other
artists. In a popular workshop exercise, writers are shown a

drawing or painting and asked to respond to it with a story of their own. This projective technique is also used by psychologists, with the Thematic Aperception Test (TAT), in order to unearth hidden personal concerns.

It reminds me that I used to do a form of this writing exercise before I even knew how to read or write. When I was a small child, I'd look at pictures in magazines—either photographs or illustrations—and tell myself stories about them. In the Christmas issue of a women's magazine my mother subscribed to, there was a reproduction of a Madonna and Child painting. Because the Infant Jesus was naked, I made up a sad little tale about a family too poor to buy clothes for their children. I even touched up the painting, imposing a happy ending by coloring in a cute little snowsuit for the baby Jesus. In Harry Crews's memoir, *A Childhood*, he recalls that he and another little boy used to make up complicated stories about the clothing models in their "Wish Book," the Sears, Roebuck catalogue.

> And before it was over, we had discovered all the connections possible between the girl in the step-ins and the young man in the knife-creased suit and the older man in the red hunting jacket with the shotguns on the wall behind him. . . . We had in the story what they thought and what they said and what they felt and why they didn't think that the young man, as good as he looked and as well as he stood in his fancy clothes, would ever straighten out and become the man the daddy wanted for his only daughter.

In his writing workshops, George Garrett uses group exercises that are

> *as zany and mind-bending as possible, designed and*
> *controlled so as to spare the exposure of the naked and*
> *raw ego. By the same token, designed, hopefully and*
> *covertly, to loosen up the kinks and muscles and some-*
> *times to prove something about the craft of writing.*

These exercises have included rewriting and "updating" Spenser's *Faerie Queen* in Tom Wolfe's style and writing letters to the (former) TV news commentator Walter Cronkite in the voice of an old lady who assumes that if she can see Walter, he can see her, too. Mona Simpson suggests the following exercises to her writing students:

- Write about the incident (real or imagined) that causes you the greatest sense of shame.
- Write about a serious argument with your parents from their point of view.
- Write from the point of view of a member of the opposite sex.

Simpson keys other exercises to reading assignments, as in the following:

- Write about a moment of sheer happiness (Stuart Dybek's "Pet Milk").
- Write the story of a person's life, from beginning to end (Flaubert's "A Simple Heart").
- Monitor your use of present and past tense consciously (Nabokov's "Spring in Fialta").

In an effort to have his fiction-writing students learn to "know" their characters, Michael Cunningham gives them a two-part assignment. First, he asks them to go out into the world and follow a stranger on the street for a while (presumably at a safe distance), carefully observing that person's physical being. Then he has them come back to class and write down twenty physical characteristics of the person followed. The first ten notations on their lists are usually obvious and superficial (blond hair, blue eyes, height, weight, etc.). But then they get to the more idiosyncratic and defining details, like the red mole on her left inner wrist or the slightly shorter leg that creates his loping gait. The results, Cunningham says, are often amazing. An accumulation of these special qualities of the flesh help the students to envision something resembling the spirit of the person observed, the equivalent of the writer's sense of his character's soul.

Here are some additional exercises recommended by other writers and teachers I know, and a few that I thought up myself:

- Write about a minor character in someone else's novel, bringing that character into the foreground of the plot. Jean Rhys did this very successfully in *Wide Sargasso Sea*, in which the first Mrs. Rochester in *Jane Eyre*— the crazy woman in the attic—tells *her* side of the story.

- Extend a favorite book into a future past its final page. What happens to Madame Bovary's little daughter, Berthe? Is she fated to follow her mother's example? Can Holden Caulfield make it in adult society?

- Do a modern riff on a period piece. Elizabeth Bennet meets computer dating. In his short story "The Kugelmass Episode," Woody Allen does a brilliant job of bringing Emma Bovary to modern-day Manhattan, where, true to character, she shops restlessly at Bloomingdale's and dreams of a career in Hollywood.

- Write a paragraph, and then rewrite it in the style of various masters: Henry James, James Joyce, Flannery O'Connor, etc. Compare these imitations with your original paragraph in an effort to recognize possible influences on your writing style.
- Test your sense of humor by cutting off the captions to various cartoons and inventing new ones to replace them; or, using just the captions, create new drawings to illustrate them.
- Write a short story entirely in dialogue. Then tell the same story without using any dialogue at all.
- Write a sentence of dialogue, conveying that it would be whispered, without adding "he (or she) whispered." Do the same thing with a sentence that would be shouted.
- Write an exchange of letters between two people who really can't communicate with each other, except on a superficial level. Be aware of the subtext of their real feelings.
- Write a paragraph about a childhood experience (real or imagined), first in the voice of the child to whom it happens, then in the voice of the adult he becomes, looking back at the event.
- Write your own obituary, bringing yourself to "life" in the process.
- Have everyone in your (long-standing) workshop write a paragraph based on a common prompt (a picture, a

sentence, or just a single word) and have one person read them all aloud. See if you can guess who wrote each paragraph.

Like works of visual art, musical composition offers certain lessons to the writer. Listening to music can teach us about harmony and counterpoint, and the instrumental or vocal solo may be usefully compared to the soliloquy in literature. With that in mind,

- Listen to a piece of music and write a fictional scene to which the music serves as a "soundtrack."

In Robert Olen Butler's *Tabloid Dreams*, each story is based on an imaginary headline from a tabloid newspaper. In a similar vein,

- Take a headline from any newspaper and write the opening paragraph to a short story, using the headline as the first sentence.

I don't often use writing exercises myself when I teach; my students are generally prolific without them. Once, I asked a group of undergraduates to eavesdrop around the campus and come back to class with some dialogue they'd overheard, written down verbatim. My plan was to have them *rewrite* it, so that it would work better, in a fictional sense. To my surprise, and theirs, everything they brought in worked very well without revision (except for a little cutting). Even the most banal conversation seemed to reveal character and contain a mini story. The *real* exercise, I decided, was simply paying attention.

I led a single-session writing workshop in a men's maximum security prison in Fairbanks, Alaska, and tried assigning a different exercise to my group of inmates. No one had brought a story to be analyzed, and I didn't want to plunge right into theory, so after a brief discussion of books we liked, I asked the men to write a paragraph or two about something that pleased them to consider. I expected that most of them would project themselves into a future in which they'd be released from confinement and living in freedom. My intention wasn't to be therapeutic. (Even in prison, a writing workshop isn't group therapy.) We had limited time together, and I figured that the subject of future happiness, on which they must have thought and dreamed at length, would kindle some spontaneous writing. They all did start writing immediately, but most of their pieces looked backward rather than forward. They wrote about childhood—a return to true innocence, I guess—and about beloved pets and indulgent grandparents. There was a sentimental sameness to the work, as if they'd been forced to remember happiness they hadn't actually known. I was sorry afterward that I hadn't just said, "Write anything that comes to mind." I think they would have gotten closer to the hard truth, as a prisoner named Jimmy Santiago Baca does, in the collection *Doing Time*, when he writes, "Most of my life I felt like a target in the crosshairs of a hunter's rifle."

I still believe that the ongoing habits of reading, listening, and watching closely, of being the kind of person, as Henry James advised, on whom nothing is ever lost, make for the best possible training any writer can get. But writing exercises can provide the additional creative stimulation you and your workshop need. It's certainly worth talking about.

21

Looking It Up

*The difference between the almost right word and the
right word is really a large matter—'tis the difference
between the lightning bug and the lightning.*

—MARK TWAIN

One of the rewards of belonging to a writing workshop is the
exchange among its members of favorite books. My own introduction to writers like Nathanael West, Leonard Gardner,
and Joanna Trollope came about that way, and in turn I was
able to spread the word to others about Henry Green, Edith
Summers Kelly, and Evan S. Connell. When I began writing this
book, I thought I'd continue the tradition by including a personal
reading list at the end. But I realize that I've already mentioned
several beloved books in previous chapters, and I'm sure I'd
leave out too many others if I tried to compile a truly comprehensive list. Instead, I'm going to recommend other kinds of

reading material that I find particularly helpful when I'm writing fiction.

First in mind, and usually nearest at hand, is my own little reference library. Its mainstay is, of course, a good dictionary, essential for definitions and spell checks. I use *Webster's New Collegiate Dictionary* because it's illustrated and has a brief encyclopedic section at the end. Carmen Gómez Plata, a gifted and scrupulous copy editor, recommends referring to two or more dictionaries because, she says, there are always discrepancies. The language keeps changing, so dictionaries of new words and of modern slang have proved to be useful, too. Two books of quotations, one classical and the other contemporary, have a permanent place on my bookshelf, because occasionally a character will quote (or misquote) Shakespeare or Groucho Marx, and I want to be sure of the content and attribution before they speak. I've collected a few foreign-language (into English) dictionaries (French, Italian, and Spanish) just in case any of my characters decides to go abroad. When I'm writing a novel, I'll refer to the almanac(s) dealing with the year(s) covered in the book, as a source of popular culture (songs, movies, etc.) and political and social events relevant to my characters and their story.

I was happy to read in an interview with Toni Morrison that she keeps a thesaurus handy in her home office. A few writers I know disdain my frequent habit of looking up synonyms. I guess they have a lengthier lexicon in their heads than I do, because sometimes the precise word or phrase I need eludes me. Searching for it is a kind of treasure hunt, and I've worn out several copies of *Roget's Thesaurus* in the process. I often discover words other than the one I'm looking for, words that can be used elsewhere at another time, so it's never a futile endeavor.

For want of space on my bookshelves and a CD-ROM on my computer, I only own a desk encyclopedia, which is well thumbed, although I'd much prefer something more comprehensive. A world atlas and a road atlas are two other staples, especially for the armchair traveler. When I was writing *Hearts* and needed to map out my characters' cross-country car trip, I referred to the road atlas for distances traveled and to discover interesting names of towns and cities. I also asked AAA, of which I'm a member, to suggest possible scenic routes the characters could follow, and a geographical dictionary provided additional, factual information about the places the characters visit.

I always keep my Bible close by, for pure reading pleasure and for all sorts of references. Many writers find the Bible and Shakespeare excellent sources of titles for their novels and stories. And a medical manual is useful whenever a character is ill, terminally or not, for looking up appropriate symptoms. (I just have to be careful to keep my old hypochondria in check!) A book of modern English usage (I use Fowler's) helps me to deal with the ongoing problems of "I" and "me," and "lay" and "lie," and one on writing style, like Strunk and White's, offers commonsense approaches to everything from punctuation to the principles of composition.

Poets & Writers, a not-for-profit organization in New York City, publishes *A Directory of American Poets and Fiction Writers* that's updated biannually; inclusion in its pages requires a published book or appearances in a variety of literary magazines. This is an excellent reference book for writers who want to contact one another and for organizations, such as libraries and schools, to find writers for readings and panel discussions. Poets & Writers often helps to subsidize these events. They also publish an excellent bimonthly magazine (called *Poets & Writers*), which gives writers without access to a local literary community the sense of belonging to a larger one. This lively, informative journal offers interviews with and essays by writers about their craft and publishing experiences. And there are regular listings of writers workshops, artists colonies, and available grants and awards. The PEN American Center, another not-for-profit organization of and for writers, publishes an entire guidebook called *Grants and Awards Available to American Fiction Writers.*

In their reflection of life, our novels and stories sometimes take us into unfamiliar territory. So it's helpful for the fiction writer to have an eclectic home library and access to all sorts of books in the public library. Like me, you may find yourself looking up things in sources as varied as medical journals, automechanics manuals, and cookbooks. The novelist who regularly reads nonfiction books, on history, psychology, sociology, and philosophy, not only gains information but broadens his experience of the world in ways that will probably deepen his own work. And I've found that reading poetry, in addition to its customary pleasures, offers lessons on both the economical and musical uses of language. The emotional charge of poems like Philip Larkin's "The Old Fools" and Elizabeth Bishop's "In the Waiting Room" is similar to the impact of an intense and compressed short story.

One last thought about books. Some of the novels, memoirs, journals, and story collections I've mentioned in previous chapters may be out of print, but there are ways of finding copies (if you're persistent), in libraries, used-book stores, through book-search services, and on the bookshelves of friends and fellow workshop members. Recently, the Authors Guild instituted something called Backinprint.com, a way for writers to sell their own extra copies of their out-of-print titles over the Internet. Maybe some of these "lost" books will officially come back into print if enough people clamor for them.

Afterthoughts

I t occurs to me now, at the end of this book, that the principles of honesty and charity I mentioned at the beginning are as essential to the writing process as they are to the success of a fiction workshop. To write honestly and to be charitable toward one's characters allows them to present their story in a believable and compelling way. And in looking over all that I've said about the complementary subjects of craft and workshops, I see that the mysterious confluence of circumstances that makes us who we are and informs what we write seems to override anything that I or anyone else can say about the art of writing fiction. We don't write just from what we know, but from the spirit of our very beings. Still, I hope that this book has been of some help and comfort to you in all of your solitary and communal efforts.

Acknowledgments

With thanks to the many writers quoted within, for their wisdom and for their generosity in writing it all down.

And with my gratitude to Caroline White, for her gifted guidance and her patience.